THE MEDIUMSHIP
OF JACK WEBBER

BY

HARRY EDWARDS

First published by Rider & Co, July 1940
Reprinted a number of times since

New Edition 2019 published by

Saturday Night Press Publications
England.
snppbooks@gmail.com
www.snppbooks.com

Format of this edition © SNPPbooks

ISBN 978-1-908421-33-3

www.snppbooks.com

Cover: *Portrait of Jack Webber by the artist, Chris Smith*
(www.chrissmithartist.co.uk.)

CONTENTS

LIST OF PHOTOGRAPHS

Leon Isaacs

Jack Webber—The Medium

OBITUARY

JACK WEBBER passed into spirit life, after a very short illness, on March 9th, 1940, aged thirty-three years.

The manuscript of this book was in the publisher's hands in January 1940.

As the book had been written while Jack Webber was still with us, and a long life of service contemplated, it has been emphasized in the Foreword and Conclusions as the mediumship was contemporary, every statement regarding the phenomena was capable of being re-demonstrated under test conditions before impartial authorities. That position has now, unfortunately been altered.

In consultation with the publishers, it was, nevertheless decided to publish the work as originally written, with the addition of this explanation.

In order to include the 1940 photographs, and in order to make the record complete, addenda have been added to various chapters.

For the interest of readers, it may be added that at no time was any weakening of the mediumship noticeable.

The number of occasions on which Mr Webber demonstrated was strictly limited and the rules were never exceeded. The Guides were frequently consulted as to the medium's physical condition, and no anxiety or hint of weakening was disclosed. Mr Webber enjoyed a strong constitution and had not had a day's illness since he was fourteen years of age, until this year.

Therefore, there is no known reason to assume that his passing was in any way connected with his mediumship.

It was only twelve days before the passing that the remarkable photograph (Plate No.7) was obtained and during the week previous to his passing he gave two very fine séances to the Spiritualist Community in London.

While the loss of the mediumship to the Spiritualist movement is great, the personal loss has been much alleviated by our knowledge of the reality of survival the evidence already received of his return (see Chapter XXII), and the many tributes to his mediumship and uplifting letters received.

His work amongst us is finished, his new work has commenced.

HARRY EDWARDS

March 30th, 1940

CHAPTER I

FOREWORD

THIS book presents a series of photographs of supernormal activity and a narrative of events incidental to them.

They have been secured through the physical mediumship of Mr Jack Webber during the fourteen months from November 1938, to December 1939. They are not ancient history, they are contemporary and are being repeated many times a year, now.

If the photographs or any statements made are challenged, it is of the utmost importance to remember that the mediumship is still functioning, and demonstrations are being continually given.[1]

No special set stage is necessary. Mr. Webber gives between one hundred and fifty and two hundred demonstrations a year, by far the greater number in places to which he is a complete stranger. As a rule, he journeys unaccompanied, so that pre-arrangement or confederacy is out of the question.

In 1939, over four thousand persons witnessed the phenomena, from small home circles to mass séances of five hundred people.

The photographs have been taken in different places, sometimes in surroundings that the medium has never before visited. Quite often he has arrived only a few minutes before the commencement of the sitting. The photographers have been official press photographers representing national newspapers who have provided their own cameras and plates and undertaken

---

1. Written before Mr Webber's passing on March 9th, 1940.

all process work in their own studios. Other persons who have taken photographs have only been present through their possessing a suitable camera.

The sitters who have been present during the period under review represent many professions, including official representatives of the British Broadcasting Corporation, National Newspapers, the Editors of the Psychic News, the *Two Worlds, Light,* and the U.S.A. *Journal of Psychical Research,* Admirals of the Fleet, Clergymen, Doctors, Scientists, University Officials etc., while Psychical Research Societies in London and the provinces have tested the mediumship over and over again.

A sceptical mind has to face the fact that the photographs and reports are true. Otherwise there must have been a gigantic conspiracy embracing many hundreds of people, including organizations and newspapers of note, all actively participating in fraudulent acts to deceive the public without motive or reward.

Newspapers and their critical representatives are only too willing to expose fraudulent mediums; yet all, without exception, have testified to the mediumship under review. No critic, worthy of the name, would classify all the alert, questioning minds that have testified to the mediumship of Jack Webber as dupes or simpletons.

To produce faked photographs, as perfect as those reproduced, would include a number of the most reputable photographic firms in the conspiracy; also the technical staffs of the newspapers whose names are printed in the reports. Actually, the question of faking negatives cannot arise since the phenomena are visible to all present when the exposure flash is made.

Finally, a hostile mind has to take into account the scores of reports published in the psychic and general Press by correspondents of unimpeachable integrity, who have voluntarily supplied appreciative commentaries on the mediumship. Numbers of these reports are included with names and dates of publication.

Three independent accounts of séances are published, two by official representatives of our national daily newspapers, reprinted word for word, and the other from the pen of one well versed in psychic research.

These give a good impression of the happenings at a typical séance.

The purpose of this book is to add a little to the known proven knowledge of the powers of the spirit people manifesting through a human medium.

Phenomena occur when the medium deliberately sits, for their manifestation in a state of deep trance and with his normal consciousness dormant. In this state of acquiescent dormancy, the right physical and mental condition for the operation is attained. Thus, an invitation is extended for the manifestations.

Every movement of matter, every vibration and radiation, even life itself, are subject to definite forces controlled by law.

The simple action of lifting an object into the air and returning it to the place from whence it came, brings into action a controlling mind force. To carry out a similar action by psychic force denotes the presence of an intelligence possessing the knowledge of applying psychic forces to a physical object. For intricate and involved operations, of which the photographs in this volume are corroborative evidence, the controlling intelligence must possess an extensive knowledge of both physical and metaphysical forces and the laws that control them.

Since no human mind is capable of manipulating, under séance or any other conditions, a medium's mind or body to produce the phenomena described, it is logical to infer that the controlling intelligence is non-human.

Such happenings cannot be the product of the medium's subconscious mind, for there has been no human experience from which a sub-conscious mind can draw such knowledge.

Therefore, if the performance of the many acts chronicled are completely outside man's comprehension, the salient fact emerges—there is no alternative—that the operating intelligence must belong to a discarnate entity, and that, therefore, spirit people do exist.

Realizing this, there is no reason why we should not accept the statements of the spirit controls—that they once lived on the earth. Unquestionable evidence is further provided by the spirit people themselves who return to their relatives in a recognizable materialized form and speak in their own voice and language of intimate mutual earth experiences. Since this is so, it is indisputable that our relatives and friends must still be "living" to be able to communicate so. If this book establishes this position its purpose will be achieved.

The value to humanity of proving beyond all doubt the truth of survival is incalculable. With the recognition that this life is but a prelude to a further and more enlightened existence, the nature of which is individual and therefore dependent upon our conduct here so must a transformation in our present code of values take place.

In this calculating and questioning age, a firm, demonstrable foundation is necessary for an enlightened philosophy of life. Never before has there been a greater need for such a philosophy than during these days of war, and the need will be even greater in the days of reconstruction after the War. All peoples will then be seeking a new morality, based upon stronger claims than traditional creedalism.

The structure of our present civilization is based upon laws determined by individual and sectional interests, pregnant with injustices, begetting wars, revolutions, and human suffering. In the past, peace efforts have been conducted by strong sectional interests, with failure as a natural result.

Peace and brotherhood, to be real, must be based upon an insistent spiritual force, founded on knowledge, recognizing the true perception of life and its purpose.

As prejudice recedes and the general acceptance of the implications of survival advances so must our civilization conform more and more to spiritual values, impelling the reconstruction of our social, economic, national, and international codes, developing life on the understanding that human effort should contribute to the peaceful, harmonious, and spiritual progress of humanity.

In other words, the aim must be to *spiritualize the world.*

.   .   .   .   .

Thanks beyond expression are due to Mr Webber for his willing co-operation in the work, and particularly so to his spirit-guides and workers for their great patience and understanding. Sometimes weeks of work on their part has been destroyed by our clumsiness—yet they have never complained. It is only when one continuously works with these spirit people that one realizes their infinity of resource and they become as personal as the closest of friends. No form of words can adequately express the thanks that are due to these wonderful people.

A tribute must be paid to Mr Leon Isaacs, for his work in applying infra-red rays to the photographing of phenomena: and the help afforded by his perfection of a practical infra-red light unit.

Thanks are also due to Mr Maurice Barbanell, Editor of the *Psychic News*, for assistance given on a number of occasions, and to the *Psychic News*, the *Two Worlds*, the *Daily Mail*, and the *Sunday Pictorial*, for the inclusion of articles and extracts taken from these journals.

HARRY EDWARDS

BALHAM PSYCHIC RESEARCH SOCIETY
N. CHILDEBERT ROAD, LONDON, S.W.17,
January 1940.

CHAPTER II

THE MEDIUM—JOHN BOADEN (JACK) WEBBER

JACK WEBBER was born of Devonshire parents at Loughor, South Wales, in 1907.

His childhood was as ordinary as that of most children, although perhaps a little more irresponsible than usual. His education was neglected during the war years in the absence of disciplinary insistence upon attendance, etc.

At the age of fourteen he commenced work in a coal mine, and continued so working until 1936. During the latter period Mr Webber would be employed underground during the day. Arriving home in the evening, he would then prepare himself to sit for physical phenomena. This dual strain on his physical resources was too great to continue, so the manual labour was given up.

In early manhood he was a cornet player in the Salvation Army band—his mother being a trenchant Salvation Army worker—whilst his father was a bell-ringer in the local Protestant church.

When Mr Webber was about twenty-one years of age, he met Miss Rhoda Bartlett, whom he married in 1930. They have two sons, Denzil, aged eight, and George, aged six.

Mrs Webber belonged to a staunch spiritualist family which, at the time when Mr Webber first met his future wife, were holding home circles for the development of their psychic gifts.

Thankful appreciation should here be mentioned of the patience and faithfulness of Mrs Webber and Mr and Mrs Evans

(Mr Webber's father and mother-in-law) for their painstaking work in developing Mr Webber, and their daughter Winnie (now Mrs Rooke), also a well-known healer, speaker, and clairvoyant.

To Mr Webber, at the age of twenty-one, spiritualism was, to use his own expression, "bunk", nevertheless, mainly in order to be with his fiancée, he attended the home circle, and was thoroughly bored with the whole procedure, invariably going to sleep.

At this period the circle sat for table phenomena, and, as is customary at such circles, messages would be tapped out. One evening Mr Webber, still a sceptic, tried to play a joke and manipulate the table to give a false message. To his surprise a message was tapped out, in spite of his mental and physical obstructive tactics. A message which, more amazing still, told of the correct place in which a lost handbag, containing money, would be found.

This incident caused Mr Webber to reconsider his former opinion of the gatherings, and he began to take a more sympathetic interest in the circles he attended.

Later on, through his Guide, information was given for the finding of the body of a man who had been missing for some days, mention being made of the actual spot by a bridge over a nearby river. On another occasion he told a friend of the passing of a workmate. They had been working together that afternoon and had parted in. good health. His friend ridiculed the idea, but afterwards it was found to be perfectly true, as the man in question had passed over at his tea-table during that same afternoon.

The table circle was changed into a circle for the development of control work, and after about two years from the commencement Mr Webber would sink into a trance-like sleep.

The next stage in the development of the medium was the control of the mind and body by spirit entities, the latter being replaced later by the controls using Mr Webber for his present-day work. This development was by no means easy, many tense moments being provided by the violence with which the controls manifested through the medium's body.

The spirit-guide in control of the medium during séances is Black Cloud. In the early days he asked for toys, musical instruments, etc., to be placed near to Mr Webber in the circle—trumpets, too, were soon added.

First of all slight movements and tappings were noted, then development came quickly and levitation of the trumpets and objects followed soon after.

It was suggested that Mr Webber should sit in a cabinet, but, to Mr Webber's normal mind to sit in an enclosed cabinet was sufficient to induce a certain amount of suspicion. Mr Webber has never used a cabinet—he prefers to be in the circle, as one of the sitters. Ropes were used to secure him to his chair in the first instance, and it is in this way that the mediumship has been built up, providing a technique the spirit-controls are accustomed to.

Researchers and others have often suggested other forms of securing the medium, including strait-jackets, sewing up in a sack, enclosing in a packing-case, etc. Such suggestions have been resisted, mainly because they would be a departure from the technique to which the controls are accustomed, secondly, because the medium should be protected from fanciful experiments that "bleed" him, and finally because the use of a red light combined with the precautions stated in the following chapter are ample and sufficient.

Even during this stage of his development Mr Webber was still sceptical as to the powers being exercised through him, and it was only after visiting other circles in the district, when the same phenomena occurred, and were testified to by independent sitters, that Mr Webber came to accept as actual fact his own psychic powers.

Very strong healing forces soon became evident, mainly through a spirit-control known as Malodar (a young Egyptian).

Considerable healing work was undertaken, including the gathering of herbs and the making of medicines therefrom. Mr Webber relates how he would be taken out into the marshlands and open country near his home, in a semi-dazed condition, to where the particular herbs grew, collecting them, and then returning home and brewing them for a special complaint. It was found that the healing work exhausted the physical body, so with the development of the physical mediumship the healing work was allowed to lapse.

ADDENDUM. MAY 1940.

Early in 1940, Mr Stanley Croft (a member of the developing circle) arrived one evening, deeply distressed. His daughter, evacuated in the Westcountry, had been admitted to hospital with severe blood poisoning, and her life was despaired of. Assistance was asked for through Mr Webber's Healing Guides, which they said they would give. Later, during the same séance, the healing control, Malodar, spoke through the trumpet and said that he had been to the patient, and that he would again return and draw the poison from her body. He also gave this evidential information—the poisoning had been caused through the sting of an insect in the head.

Up to this time, the cause of the poisoning had not been traced, and the medical authorities had no knowledge of the cause of the trouble. Mr Croft wrote and inquired whether such a sting could be traced. It was then recalled that a day or so before the illness, a bee had become enmeshed in Miss Croft's hair and had stung her when it was being extricated. Neither Miss Croft nor her mother had associated the sting of the bee with the illness, and this evidential information proves the powers of diagnosis, and which, of course, could not possibly have been telepathy.

In a few days, all traces of the poison left the patient and the recovery was complete.

Most remarkable, was the manner in which healing oils would be produced from the medium's hands. Mr Webber would stand by his patient in an entranced state and thick oil would ooze on to his hands. So thick were these oils that his hands presented the appearance of having been immersed in a large can of Vaseline. The patient would then be massaged with the oil.

The preparation of the medium for the work ahead was not restricted to the developing circles. It continued at night-time, when loud knocks would be heard, the bed-clothes would be pulled off the bed, a bedside table on which stood a paraffin lamp and other odds and ends would tip over sideways and descend to the floor without any oil being spilled or an object displaced—and then be righted again. Voices would be heard, and often Mr Webber would forcefully express himself, telling the controls to leave him alone.

Gradually, as the years passed by, the powers developed, voices in the trumpets, and independent of the trumpet, became stronger. Heads and hands materialized, and eventually the medium was prevailed upon to give demonstrations before strangers, visiting on a friendly basis the homes of neighbouring spiritualists.

Until quite recently Mr Webber was afraid of these phenomena. Generally, as soon as he sat for a séance and the light was extinguished, and before Mr Webber went into a trance, there would be noises and the levitation of trumpets, etc. These made the medium fearful until the trance state took away his consciousness. However, this fear is now disappearing, for in the developing circle, in red light, voice and levitation have been manifested before normality departs. At first these phenomena were of a few seconds duration, and then week by week they became gradually prolonged to from five to ten minutes, consequently the medium can now see a part of the phenomena, and is able to hear and speak to his own controls.

Mr Webber is an unassuming man, unlettered, fond of athletic sports, a keen dart player, and always willing to help anyone in need of his assistance. Never yet has any person been denied who needed the comfort of the "return" of their loved ones, even if they were unable to pay as much as a portion of the usual fee. Mr Webber has co-operated with cheerful willingness in all efforts to furher our knowledge of the spirit people.

The following are some of the main spirit-controls concerned in the present-day mediumship.

Black Cloud. A North American Indian of the Mohawk tribe. He takes charge of the séance and is in direct control of the medium's body. When Black Cloud first made his presence known he could not speak English, and left for a time to learn, through a medium, an English vocabulary. It is to Black Cloud that we are most indebted, both for his co-operation in taking photographs and also for the considerate understanding which he has shown, and which has endeared him to those who have had the privilege of co-operating in the work.

Paddy. A boy control. He is one of the most active workers in the séance, and is in control of the "inner" circle. He acts as instructor to the spirit people who desire to make their presence known, telling them the way to use the ectoplasmic voice mechanism. He has an exceedingly humorous turn of mind, but can be very serious, especially when giving an explanation as to how the phenomena are produced. Paddy sings in a thin voice and has materialized many times. He is a constant visitor to the homes of members of the developing circle, recounting various incidents that have happened to them during the day. A most lovable personality.

Reuben. A South American, schoolmaster by profession, visited this country during his earthly life and passed over from tetanus. In his early attempts to control the medium was very violent, reproducing the physical contortions of the disease from which he passed over. He is a powerful agency in the circle work, and is particularly noted for his strong singing voice, a rich baritone, which has been recorded by the Decca Record Co.,

Ltd. This voice is so powerful as to be of full loudspeaker strength and is referred to in a later chapter. Reuben also controls the medium for trance addresses on the platform, but this work has been allowed to lapse in order to conserve the medium's strength. He has fully materialized.

Other controls are Malodar, the healer; Talgar; Rev. John Boaden (a great-uncle of the medium); Dr Millar and Professor Dale, whose work is mainly concerned with the materializations and whose earthly existences have been verified from the data they have supplied.

PLATE 2. THE DEVELOPING CIRCLE IN LONDON
From left to right: Mrs & Mr Harry Edwards, Mr Stanley Croft, Mr & Mrs Jack Webber, Mr Jack McCulloch, Mr James Evans, Mrs Gladys Layton.

CHAPTER III

INFRA-RED PHOTOGRAPHY

THE following is a simple non-technical description of the method whereby the photographs reproduced in this book have been secured.

All the photographs have been taken by means of infra-red ray. By this means the lens of a camera is able to record in the dark whatever is in existence as clearly and as precisely as a photograph taken in normal white light.

The method adopted has been to flash a powerful Sashalite bulb housed in a light-proof cabinet. One side of the cabinet is fitted with an infra-red filter.

The bulb generates from 100,000 to 150,000 watts, and the period of the flash, and therefore the exposure, is from one-fiftieth to one-seventy-fifth part of a second.

With this momentary flash of such tremendous power only a very dim, dull-red light emission is seen by the eye.

The cameras are loaded with plates sensitive to the infra-red ray.

When the infra-red ray first became practical for photographic use in the dark, it was said that it would expose séance-room trickery. Through Mr Webber's mediumship it has proved the genuineness of physical phenomena, and, by doing so, has provided evidence of survival after "death".

The infra-red ray is most suitable for this work: firstly, because the radiations emitted are least harmful to ectoplasmic formations, etc. (such formations cannot be physically created in the presence of ultra-violet rays, which are harmful to mediumship); and secondly, because it is the only known process permitting photographic records to be taken in darkness.

The rapidity of the exposure prevents the possibility of collusion by any sitter with the medium, for any change of position would be recorded.

As a general rule a number of cameras are positioned in the room in order to obtain photographs from different angles. Any person with a camera possessing a reasonably fast lens can take the photographs.

The majority of these photographs have been taken during the sitting of Mr Webber's developing circle, or at special photographic séances, when representatives of the Press and other organizations have been present in their official capacity, bringing with them their own equipment. Occasionally they have been taken in places which the medium has never before visited.

Generally the Guide, speaking through the medium, gives the instruction when the photograph is to be taken, and the operator in charge of the Infra-red flash then presses the switch. The camera lenses have meanwhile remained open, awaiting the necessary exposure. On one occasion the press-switch to fire the bulb was placed under the medium's hand, so that the Guide in control of the medium could press the switch and so take the photograph at the most suitable moment.

CHAPTER IV

THE SECURING OF THE MEDIUM

THE general method of securing the medium is by a rope, fifteen yards long, to a wooden armchair of the Windsor pattern. On occasion the rope has been provided by independent people. Sometimes short lengths are used, with additional independent tapes and threads to secure the arms and legs.

The tying-up can be carried out by any person present. At the hundreds of public séances the roping has been carried out by skilled tiers, sailors, policemen, and psychic researchers, etc.

Further precautions employed are the sewing-up of the ends of the rope, after tying, thus making it endless. The ends and knots are sealed with wax and impressed with a seal provided by any sitter. A piece of cotton or wool is then tied at the base of one thumb, a piece of paper threaded on through a needle-hole, and the other end tied to the base of the opposite thumb. The value of this precaution in demonstrating supernormal activity is seen when two or three objects are in simultaneous levitation, so wide apart from each other that it would be a physical impossibility for the medium to accomplish the movement normally with hands secured by a cotton or a piece of fragile wool, fifteen inches long. The distancing of the objects in levitation can be so wide apart that no one person could manipulate both movements, even with hands quite free.

On a number of occasions at the London Spiritual Alliance in 1939, a very long rope (the property of the organization) was used, in which the roping was carried out to plan. A reef-knot first secured the centre of the rope to the back of the chair. The rope was then passed round the body four times, and each time knotted at the back of the chair. Each upper arm was twice bound and knotted to the back strut of the chair, and the forearms were bound several times to the arm-rest. The remainder of the rope secured the medium's legs and ankles to the chair legs. The ends of the rope were then sewn together with strong thread, sealed with wax, and impressed with a signet-ring. On these occasions (as often happens) the ropes were tied just sufficiently tight so as not to impede blood circulation. During the course of a sitting (about two hours) the arms and legs swell, so that by the time the séance ends the ropes are pressing well into the flesh, so much so that the rope-marks are visible hours after the termination of the sitting.

At the sittings with the London Spiritual Alliance full demonstrations were given, of which the following two incidents are worthy of mention.

Mr Webber was roped as above, his own rope being left loose near at hand. During the séance this spare rope was taken and the sitter next to the medium was roped by unseen "hands" to his chair. The rope was, taken right across the circle and intertwined in the chair of the sitter opposite, under the seat and round the chair legs, the rope returning to further enmesh the first sitter, the remainder being tied in a confusion of knotting with no end visible. When the séance was over the rope had to be cut to free the sitter and to free the rope from each chair.

The second incident occurred on another occasion, the medium being similarly roped. When the coat was removed from the body while the medium's hands were held by adjacent sitters, it was found that an elastic armlet the medium wore above the elbow was outside a rope, that is, the rope that had been tied over the coat in the first tying up was underneath the elastic arm-band. To do this normally, the end of the sewn and sealed rope must have been freed, all knotting undone to the armband and then threaded through, the knotting and binding restored and the ends sewn up, and sealed with the signet ring of the sitter. Later on, when the coat was returned to the medium's body, the rope was freed from the armlet and left *outside* the coat as originally tied. The Guide later explained that the armlet had been dematerialized when the coat was taken off and rematerialized outside the rope; when the coat was being replaced the process had to be reversed to enable the rope to be freed to be placed outside the coat.

Another method that has been used is to employ "sensitive" roping, so that if the medium ever (normally) freed himself from the ropes they would fall into one loop, impossible to replace without assistance.

Repeatedly during séances, the white light is put on immediately before and after some phase of phenomena requiring rapid action. Those who roped the medium are invited by the Guide to examine the ropes, etc., to see if they are precisely as originally tied. The roping has never been found to have altered, and at the end of a séance; whatever the phenomena may have been, it is exactly as tied in the beginning. The report later on by Mr Colin Evans of one of our séances illustrates this point in detail.

Roping, no matter how elaborately tied, is ineffective to keep the medium in the chair, if the Guide wishes to take him out of the bonds. This feat is one of the most remarkable of those exhibited by the spirit people. The *modus operandi* is as follows: the light is put on to show the medium roped in the chair, the ropes and knots are examined, and the light is switched off. The next one hears is the instruction for "light" which shows the medium standing on the far side of the circle. The time which has elapsed may be only a few seconds. The ropes are seen to be resting on the chair as tied, even to the crossing of one rope over another, in precisely the same position as if the medium's body was within them. In considering this process it is interesting to remember that as a rule it takes two people from two to four minutes each to tie the medium in the ropes alone, and an appreciable time to undo the knotting, sometimes longer, especially when the knots are obstinate, than the time taken to tie him up.

The return of the medium to the roped condition in the chair is also a matter of seconds, from five to ten. The medium is seen standing in an entranced condition away from the chair. Before the light is put out, he may be seen to be gyrating quickly. The light is extinguished, and a slight sound may be heard. There is an immediate call for light, and he is seen back in his chair, roped precisely, to the minutest detail, as before.

A variation of the above is as follows:

The white light is put on and the ropings are examined. Then two sitters are asked to hold the medium's hands. The light is extinguished. The sitters linked to the medium feel his hands fall over the side of the chair arm and the medium rises to his feet, out of the ropes, without exertion or jerkiness.

On several occasions the medium has been levitated out of the ropes and deposited outside the circle of sitters. The sitters are close together, touching each other with their hands linked, in circle formation. The medium therefore had to be levitated into the air and carried over the sitters' heads to enable him to alight outside the circle. Sometimes on such an occasion he may be suspended in the air for a number of minutes, his feet gently resting on the shoulders of a sitter who is asked by the Guide to place his hands on them and to feel up the sides of the legs. While the sitter is doing this the ceiling may be somewhat violently knocked by the medium's head and or hands. The interesting feature of this phenomena is that no weight is felt on the sitter's shoulders. The medium is then brought to the floor outside the circle of sitters. As a rule, this takes place at the end of a séance, and the medium is then brought to himself—standing. When this occurs, the ropes are left on the chair, and efforts are made by one of the sitters to try and get into the roping. A lady and the author, both smaller boned than Mr Webber, have unsuccessfully tried to place both arms and legs into the fastenings. Struggling takes place for a number of minutes, but even after taking the shoes off, no one has yet succeeded in doing it. When one has been able to get one arm in it was only by displacing the ropes and rocking one's clothing. Rarely is it possible to get the coat-sleeves under the ropes at all, and when the medium's upper arm was bound to the chair the task of normal re-entry was absolutely impossible. These normal efforts made considerable noise, and it is noteworthy that when the medium is returned to the roped condition in the chair, all that is heard is one slight movement as the levitated body comes to rest on the chair accompanied by an immediate request for "light."

In June 1939 three representatives of the British Broadcasting Corporation were present. They were Mr Lot de Biniere, Director of Outside Broadcasts, and Mr John Snagge and Mr Michael Standing, Commentators. These gentlemen undertook the securing of the medium. After he had been roped, the ends of the ropes, knots, etc., were bound with cotton and knotted. An extra length of cotton was tied by Mr Lot de Biniere round the outside of the medium's forearm to the arm-rest of the chair, then tied round the buttons on the coat cuff, carried straight in front of the medium's body to the other side where the opposite coat cuff buttons, arm, and chair were similarly secured. During this séance the coat was taken off while the medium's hands were held by two of these gentlemen, without the cotton being broken (examination being made in white light immediately after the coat fell to the floor). Later, the coat was returned to the body with the cotton intact and knotted around the coat cuff buttons as originally tied. At the end of a two-hours' séance, Mr Lot de Biniere was asked to thoroughly examine the cotton on the ropes and especially that in front of the body, and he declared that everything was exactly as originally tied. The Guide then asked him to break the cotton in front of the medium, which he did with negligible effort. This demonstrated how the slightest tension on the cotton during the evening's phenomena would have easily broken the strand.

Later experiments include the tying (after roping) of silk threads, firmly and tightly around the wrists and to the chair (knots underneath) and elbow to the back of the chair (knots at rear). At the end of the séance the silk thread was found to be embedded in the flesh of the wrist owing to swelling.

In other chapters different methods of securing the medium are referred to.

To those who still may consider that the medium may possess a technique to permit his exit and entry from the fastenings normally, there is a final aspect that forbids that supposition. At the commencement of a séance, immediately after the tying, the light is put out. Within a fraction of a second one or two trumpets are in levitation encircling the sitters. As the levitation ends and the trumpets come to the floor, there is an immediate request for light. The trumpets may have moved several feet away from the medium and have come to rest well away from his chair. Frequently in most séances the trumpets are lying on the floor, in positions where it is absolutely impossible for the medium to touch them without getting out of the fastenings and reaching down to pick them up. The almost instantaneous switching-on of the light before and after this, and other phenomena, illustrates beyond any possible doubt whatever that supernormal means must have been employed. The Guides have so perfected this rapidity of action that trumpets are often seen moving as the light goes on—and still more amazing, continuing in motion for a period while the light is on. (See the description by Colin Evans of a séance, further on in this volume.)

The main purpose of roping is the prevention of any conscious or subconscious action on the part of the medium, but it is also designed to satisfy the sitters the medium is not consciously, subconsciously, or fraudulently producing movement. The one aim of the mediumship is to provide proof of survival through supernormal action, directed by intelligences possessing a greater knowledge than we have.

Special sittings in red light add further testimony to the powers of the spirit people in manipulating forces beyond human knowledge. In red light levitation has been repeatedly observed—the medium meanwhile being bound in his chair, while articles, trumpets, etc., are moving round, up and down, twisting, turning, and performing all kinds of evolutions without any visible connection with the medium. Alternatively, the article is seen sometimes in movement, strongly held by an ectoplasmic structure emerging from the solar plexus or other part of the medium's body—the medium being seen, quite still, roped in his chair. (See later chapter on ectoplasmic structures.)

CHAPTER V

REPORT OF A SÉANCE BY BERNARD GRAY
(*Sunday Pictorial*).

THE séance reported took place on May 24th, 1939, and occupied two pages of the *Sunday Pictorial* dated May 28th, 1939·

Mr Gray prefaced his report with an affidavit as follows:

"I, BERNARD GRAY, of 27, Barn Rise, Wembley Park, in the County of Middlesex, Journalist, make Oath and say as follows:

" 1. That my description of the incidents enumerated in the Article written by me hereunto annexed and marked 'B.G.' to appear in the issue of the *Sunday Pictorial* of the Twenty-eighth day of May One thousand nine hundred and thirty-nine under the heading of' I Swear I Saw This Happen' is true.

"2. I further make Oath and say that the incidents so described in such Article did occur in my presence."

This oath was sworn before a solicitor yesterday.

I bound him to his chair, hand and foot, with knots and double knots which a sailor once taught me.

Just to make sure he couldn't wriggle out and back without my knowing it, I tied lengths of household cotton from the ropes to the chair legs. And I sewed up the front of his jacket with stout thread.

So began my second investigation into the mysteries of Spiritualism.

The man I had trussed up was Jack Webber, formerly a Welsh miner. He's now a medium—a man for whom such remarkable claims are made that I selected him for my first test.

Through him, I was told, are performed some of the most astonishing miracles of spirit power, physical demonstrations intended to prove the reality of life after death.

And in this, my second adventure into Spiritualism during my association with the *Sunday Pictorial*, I want physical phenomena.

Startling deeds, not words, as proof. Not testimonies of people claiming to be healed, not messages from the dead. Just material facts which a materially minded man like me can grasp.

I want final and complete conviction. That is more important to me than Hitler, the Axis, or even the threat of war. And that is why I have asked the Editor to allow me—for a while—to leave politics, and go in search of Truth.

. . . . .

So we sat, fourteen of us, a cheerful, talkative group of very ordinary people, in a plainly furnished room at Balham, London.

There was a Metropolitan policeman. A consulting engineer. A waiter. A postman. A foreman plumber. Several women of various ages. And next to me, between the medium and me, Mr Harry Edwards, leader of the Balham Psychic Society, by trade a printer.

We all held hands loosely, Mr Webber settled himself back as comfortably as my knots would allow, and out went the light, leaving only a red bulb gleaming dully through the darkness from the middle of the room.

Things began to happen immediately. They went on happening with remarkable rapidity, with startling variety, for ninety minutes.

But I do not want to recount them in order. For I want to describe first two astonishing happenings which make the rest seem small in contrast. Happenings which I, personally, can only compare with the miracles of the New Testament.

.   .   .   .   .

THERE WAS THE APPEARANCE, IN MID-AIR, SO TO SPEAK, OF A PERFECT HUMAN FACE.

I am sitting, remember, only one removed from the medium. An hour of the séance has gone by. The early tenseness, the trace of excitement, which perhaps affected me at the start has disappeared.

I am my normal, cool, and vigilant self—alert for any sign of deception, accustomed to the eerie glimmer of light we get from the red bulb near the ceiling.

In the corner, so near I can touch him, the medium is breathing heavily, gulping occasionally, moaning uneasily at times, like a man with a nightmare.

Suddenly, he gurgles alarmingly, as if making some still greater effort.

Before me rises a kind of tablet, rather like a slate, and from the upper surface it sheds a luminous white light.

I watch it intently, not in the least perturbed. I saw it in its normal state before the séance started. An ordinary piece of four-ply wood, about a foot long and nine inches wide.

Now it hovers in front of the medium's face, its soft radiance lighting his features so clearly I can see the closed eyes and the twitching lips.

It moves gently down to his hands and I see quite clearly that the arms are still bound to the chair.

"IT'S SHOWING YOU THE MEDIUM TO CONVINCE YOU HE'S STILL IN THE SAME POSITION," MR. EDWARDS EXPLAINS, IN A NORMAL TONE. "AH! YOU'RE REALLY GOING TO SEE SOMETHING NOW!"

The glowing tablet has moved over to me. It hangs motionless so close to my face I feel that if I breathe hard I shall blow it away.

"Watch!" says Mr Edwards, giving my hand a squeeze.

Then above the tablet I begin to see something white emerging from the darkness. Almost invisible at first, it grows stronger every moment, like a motor car headlamp advancing through fog; until I can clearly see it as a diaphanous ellipse, standing on its end, as it were, on the tablet.

"Ectoplasm," says Mr Edwards. "Watch closely in the centre of it!"

No need to tell me. My eyes are glued on it, though, I want to emphasize, I'm still cool and unemotional.

Now, framed in this luminous halo, I can perceive dimly what appear to be features. They are becoming clearer, easier to trace. There's the nose, and—yes—the mouth. The eyes, and, my God! The eyelids are moving.

The tablet moves still closer. The eyes, soft and natural, are looking directly into mine. I jerk myself back to a detached, inquisitive state of mind, examine the thing in front of me closely and searchingly.

It's not like the pictures of spirit faces many of us have seen in Spiritualist papers. It's not white and unearthly, like the frame in which it is set. RATHER IT IS A HUMAN FACE—BUT SOFTER, FINER, AND SOMEHOW DIFFERENT.

I can trace the cheek-bones fading back from the eyes. The lips, they are quite clear. The chin, rounded and delicate, is silhouetted against the lower rim of the halo.

I recognize it suddenly as the face of a very old lady. Just like a lovely miniature—for it is much smaller, now I come to think, than the face of any human adult.

"Try and speak to us," says Mr Edwards, encouragingly.

I am watching the lips. They part a little, move with an effort.

There's a whisper. What is she saying? Who is she speaking to? Yes—I've got it.

"MY BOY, MY BOY," WHISPERS A WOMAN'S VOICE, IN THE TONE A WEALTH OF LOVE, OR MAYBE COMPASSION.

"Who's she speaking to?" I ask, without taking my eyes off the face for a second.

"You," replies Edwards. "Speak to her!"

"Who are you?" I ask, gently.

"I am——," she answers, and whispers a name I shall not repeat—it is personal.

"I cannot stay," she goes on. "I just want you all to see me. God bless you, my boy . . ."

The tablet and its burden move away. I can see it floating around our circle. Other sitters are exclaiming that they can see it, quite plainly, that it's wonderful.

I'M GLAD I'M NOT THE ONLY ONE WHO CAN SEE IT . . .

The tablet returns to me. The features in the miniature are fading, like outlines yielding to the dusk of a summer evening. Now the halo is going too.

Only the tablet is left. Its gleam disappears with the suddenness of a light being extinguished. The tablet falls with a clatter at my feet.

"Lights on," says a voice instantly.

There's the click of a switch. In less than five seconds the whole room is bathed in electric light. Everybody is in his or her place, holding hands.

The medium is bound just the same in his chair unconscious in his trance.

AND AT MY FEET IS THE BIT OF COMMON FOUR-PLY WOOD . . .

The deep voice which comes from the medium's corner—they call it the voice of Black Cloud, Webber's Indian spirit "guide"—says :

"I want the gentleman sitting next to Mr Edwards to hold the medium's right hand. I want the lady on the left of the medium to hold his left hand."

Edwards guides my hand over his knees to the hand of the medium. I feel my fingers seized in a powerful grasp. The pressure tightens till it hurts. I set my teeth and wait.

The medium is moaning like a man in pain.

I can feel a soft fabric rubbing against my wrist. "Can you feel his coat?" asks the deep voice in the corner.

"I can feel some kind of material on my wrist," I answer, readily.

"I am dematerializing his coat and taking it off."

Now the coat is rubbing the other side of my wrist. Something drops to the floor with a light, rustling impact.

"LIGHTS ON," SAYS THE VOICE SHARPLY.

Simultaneously, it seems, somebody presses the switch.

The medium is in his shirt-sleeves. He is no longer wearing his coat. Round his arms, over his shirt now, are the ropes, still fastened by my patent knots.

The thin strands of cotton from the ropes to the chair are unbroken.

On the floor, the medium's jacket. Not a stitch holding the edges together broken. My twisted thread round the button just as I had left it.

"That is merely intended to prove to you that the spirit world exists and has power to dematerialize," says the deep voice in the corner, when the lights are off again. "Later I hope to replace the medium's coat."

Half an hour later the lady on the other side and I are asked to hold Webber's hands a second time. Again the grip is firm enough to be painful.

A rustling. Cloth rubbing against my wrist again. Yes, and now the other side.

Lights. Webber is wearing his coat once more. Over and round each arm, the bonds. The cotton intact. The thread just as before. BUT THE BONDS AND THE COTTON ARE OVER THE COAT.

"My hand was gripped by his all the time," says the girl across from me, rubbing her fingers. "And I felt the coat go through my wrist. Didn't you?"

.　　　.　　　.　　　.　　　.

Well, those two happenings, or miracles—call them what you like, take a bit of explaining away.

There were other things too. Heaps of them.

"I can feel a hand on my head," said Mr Edwards, casually, just as if it were quite a natural thing for a hand to emerge from nowhere.

"I can feel something on my head," I said a moment later, and gripped Edwards's hand more tightly to make sure it hadn't been raised.

Something was pulling my hair pretty hard. I realized then with a sense of shock that the "something" was definitely fingers, yet rather different from human fingers. They felt sharper, more like claws, seemed almost metallic at the tips.

My neighbour chuckled.

"I know what they're doing," he said, highly amused.

The fingers pulled me firmly by the hair in Edwards's direction, till my head was touching his. My hair was pulled and twisted about for fully a minute. "We're being tied together," said my neighbour, laughing. "Can't you feel your hair being twisted with mine?"

We were tied together, too! We couldn't separate, and the séance was held up for a moment or two while the lights were put on so that we could be unravelled.

"A mischievous trick," said everybody else, laughing at our plight. Mischievous, all right. Inexplicable, too. I'll swear nobody moved before, during, or after the knots were tied in our hair.

Frequently throughout the proceedings the luminous trumpets were shooting about the room three at a time, with the speed and accuracy of swallows in flight.

"I should like to be absolutely sure nobody is holding them," I said boldly, though I myself considered it impossible.

One of the trumpets shot straight at my head with the speed of an express train, pulled up sharp just as it touched my temple, and I cringed expecting a knock-out blow.

That tin cone proceeded to run itself on my face and round my head, pressing first the broad end, then the narrow end, against my lips to prove it had no earthly connection at any point on its surface.

A bell which I'd seen on a table in a corner rose into the air and rang a rhythmic accompaniment to our singing. A pair of clappers, similar to those used by a dance band drummer, floated about clacking merrily in time with the music.

In a powerful bass voice, which has been recorded on gramophone discs, "Reuben" led some of the singing. Toys in the room, illuminated by a strange incandescent glow, leapt from the table and sailed about near the ceiling.

A boy, I was told, plays with the toys—a boy who died some years ago.

As something moved off the table and began to dart about the room, Mr Edwards explained that it was a doll.

Whatever it was, it settled on my knee, and frolicked up and down my leg. I could feel it as well as see it glowing, like an outsize glow worm. It came to rest finally on my knee. And when the lights came on, I found that it was indeed a toy elephant, such as any child would use in play.

You see therefore, it wasn't a gloomy gathering by any means. The strange pranks with the toys—a clockwork engine wound itself up and ran itself down near the ceiling—distinctly enlivened the proceedings.

All these little things, however, paled into insignificance beside a remarkable demonstration of furniture removing by unseen hands.

THE HEAVY TABLE IN THE CORNER, JUST BEHIND ME, ROSE STRAIGHT UP INTO THE AIR, BRUSHING MY COAT AS IT PASSED. IT SETTLED ONE LEG LIGHTLY ON MY SHOULDER FOR A MOMENT, WAS WAFTED RIGHT OVER TO THE OTHER SIDE OF THE ROOM AND DESCENDED TO THE FLOOR WITH A DISTINCT BANG.

I saw it in passage, because it was outlined against the red light.

And of course there were spirit messages for some of the sitters. I do not want to write about them. In this series of articles, I am concerned more with incidents.

Well, that is my testimony.

I cannot explain anything I saw.

BUT EVERY WORD I HAVE WRITTEN IS TRUE.

And although many of my friends will think I've gone crazy—I say again: I SAW IT HAPPEN.

CHAPTER VI

CRITICAL ANALYSIS OF A SÉANCE BY
COLIN EVANS, B.A.

I ATTENDED a group séance for physical phenomena with Jack Webber, on Monday, February 27th, 1939. I was particularly alertly observant and more analytical and critical than, in my own experience as a medium, it is usually advisable to be (owing to the unhelpful mental radiations resulting from such an attitude).

The only two sitters who might be supposed to have personal association with the medium or whom even a hostile sceptic might suspect of collusion, were Mr Harry Edwards, the head of the Balham Psychic Research Society—under whose auspices Webber sits—and Webber's father-in-law. These two gentlemen were at points in the room most remote from the medium—the former at the very opposite end of the room, the latter in the diagonally opposite corner furthest from Webber, where the electric light control is. No phenomena occurred near enough to either of these gentlemen for it to be physically possible for them to play any part in it, and at no time, by any possible means, could either of them have left his position without the full knowledge of half the independent sitters. Neither of these gentlemen had any part in the roping and tying of the medium or the stitching of his coat.

I sat by the door in the fourth seat from the medium. This séance was held in darkness.

I scrutinized very closely the tying of the medium's arms and ankles to the chair by rope. Two men did this, and the knots tied and the tightness of the rope were such that no "escape" trickery was possible that would permit of getting back into the ropes without obvious disturbance of them. They cut closely into the flesh, and the muscles of arms and ankles were immovably secured to the solid wood of the chair, so that absolutely no movement of the feet or of the arms above the wrist was possible; and I made special note (without drawing attention to it) of the exact angle at which two looped portions of rope crossed one another under the forearm. Even had it been possible to slip the arm from this rope, and later to put it back, it would have been an utter and complete impossibility to arrange precisely the same angle of crossing of the rope there, except by using both hands to do so, and to be able to see clearly while doing it—and therefore an utter impossibility for the medium himself to achieve, in light or in darkness, or for any other person to accomplish in the dark.

Before he was tied in the chair, his coat was stitched all down the front so that it was an absolutely tight fit that could not possibly be taken off or put on again, even if his arms had been free, without undoing the stitching. I examined the stitching, and noted "trappy" ways it was caught and twisted round certain buttons that would have "given away" any interference made by resewing. After the seance, it took some minutes to cut away this stitching with scissors.

The first movement of the trumpets occurred instantly on the light being put out. By "instantly" I mean an interval of about one-tenth of a second—judging that minute interval of time by my experience as a photographer fairly familiar with speeded camera shutters and exposures. These trumpets—about two feet in height and two in number and very plentifully daubed with luminous paint so that they were never lost sight of—had been standing on the floor well out of reach of the medium's hands where he was seated. First one trumpet soared swiftly up into the air, and then both trumpets simultaneously a moment later. The direction in which each trumpet pointed, and its angle and the position of the unilluminated narrow ends could be quite accurately judged from the luminous portions owing to the distinctive shape of the luminous paint on the aluminium.

They rose vertically till the broad ends were about three feet from the floor, then tilted over horizontally, and, mostly with the narrow ends towards the medium, moved freely in all directions away from him to distances of seven or eight feet (from the nearest part of the medium's chair to the broad ends of the trumpets, leaving about five or six feet between the nearest part of the medium's chair and the narrow end of the trumpets), but occasionally turned completely round and moved equally freely with the broad ends pointing towards him and the narrow ends away from him. No mechanical device of the nature of a rod or tongs could have produced this effect by any human possibility.

They repeatedly tapped firmly on the bodies of the sitters, including myself, and on the medium's own head and body, and later in the séance soared to the full height of the room—about twelve or thirteen feet—knocking against the ceiling in the middle of the room, and against the walls at considerable distances from the medium, and sometimes at such distances from one another that no one person could simultaneously have been manipulating both trumpets, even if free to walk about and stand on chairs or the like.

Repeatedly the medium's control called for "light" and every time the light was switched on instantly, and as it was switched on the trumpets would sink with a fairly rapid movement, but not so rapid as a falling body, unsupported, towards the floor, and when the light was on the trumpets were usually just reaching the floor, but still in movement, and continued moving for a moment or two—once for almost half a minute—with gentle movements, obviously intelligently controlled, on the floor—not rolling on their curved sides, but "hopping" as it were on their broad flat ends.

Every time the light was in this way flashed on suddenly, the medium was seen to be still securely roped and tied with the knots and the exact angle of the crossing loops of rope so undisturbed as to prove that he had not even been twitching restlessly as a medium in trance often does, and this within a small fraction of a second of movements of the trumpets at a distance from his body that could not have been normally manipulated unless he had been free from the ropes. His hands were empty and there was no possibility of his having concealed any mechanical device for moving the trumpets at a distance.

Two luminous plaques were, first separately and then simultaneously, levitated in the same way as the trumpets, and levitated to a position, once, where their light shone clearly on the motionless and helplessly-tied-up medium and neighbouring sitters, showing their complete independence of the medium's and sitters' bodies. Incidentally all sitters' hands were linked throughout the seance. These plaques or luminous slates fell flat to the floor after each levitation of them, at considerable distances (from four feet and upwards) away from the medium's chair. Several times the moment the light had been switched off again, the flat luminous-painted slabs of wood in question rose immediately from the floor in a way that would not have been possible normally without some person reaching down to the floor to pick them up or using tongs or some such device to reach them, and when there had been no time even for a person not tied or held or restrained or controlled in any way to make such movement.

I satisfied myself that the least movement in or from his chair, or of his chair, even tilting or tipping it in any direction, would make a clearly distinguishable sound and no such sound was heard at any time during the séance.

A tambourine and some bells were visibly (all luminous) and audibly levitated and "played" at heights of seven or eight feet from the floor and in the centre of the room, six or seven feet from the medium, floating to that position from a table near the medium's chair instantly on light being switched off, and remaining in motion at the distances mentioned up to the very moment of light being switched on again. This occurred repeatedly, as did every phenomenon produced.

Two pairs of castanets or clappers, also luminous, were levitated to the centre of the room and to a height of some ten feet—nearly to the ceiling—and for about three minutes played in strict time and tempo, very strongly, to the rhythm of the sitters' singing. These dropped to the floor from "mid-air" at the moment of light being switched on.

Once, the very instant light was switched off after I had scrutinized the undisturbed tying of the medium in his chair, and while all sitters' hands were linked, materialized hands, absolutely solid, warm, and objective, and obviously "living flesh" tapped my forehead and cheeks and rested on my forehead and the back of my head, or tapped my shoulders and my knees. Ladies on both sides of me reported the same thing, and so did sitters all round the room—once or twice this phenomenon was reported simultaneously from widely separated parts of the room.

A lady, whom I know very slightly, but whom I definitely know to be a regular and experienced fee-paying sitter with many mediums when she is in England (she is not English and is often abroad), and who can hardly be suspected of confederacy, reported child hands clasping hers. As she was linking hands with two other sitters (strangers) at the time, one of these gentlemen also felt the child's hands simultaneously on his own. The child then spoke in the direct voice. Its name was correctly given and it was accepted as an evidential materialization of the lady's "dead" little girl, who she declared had never manifested before and who she also declared was not known of as having ever existed to the medium or sitters in the séance.

Two dead friends spoke to me in the direct voice through the trumpet. Neither of them gave absolutely arguable evidence of identity, but I feel satisfied that I knew them both. Their voice and intonation and manner of speech differed from one another and both of them from the medium in a way that to me was absolute proof of the complete impossibility of mimicry, and the voices were clearly within a few inches of my face, and could not have issued from the medium's lips without at least six people knowing he had left the chair to which he was roped. The messages showed evidential knowledge of health conditions of my own which are not obvious and not public knowledge nor, as far as I can tell, knowable by Webber.

Another lady was spoken to, at an even greater distance from the medium, in the same way by a spirit who gave the full christian and surname of Phyllis Gunning, which she accepted as evidential. This name was not mentioned until a spirit uttered it.

Other sitters also received in direct voice what they accepted as good personal evidence. Voices and accents were well differentiated.

After the medium had been inspected and his ropes and knots and stitched coat had been examined in full white light, the light was switched off and afterwards switched on again. The medium was seen to be still tightly and securely roped in his chair, the rope (including the evidentially exact angle at which these two loops crossed *under* one arm, which the medium himself could not have seen or rearranged even had the rope been loose enough for him to get his arms free and replace them) undisturbed—*his coat was off.* The stitching of the coat was examined and was undisturbed. The light was switched off again, and on being switched on again *he was again wearing the coat*, the sleeves being perfectly straight and smooth to a degree impossible if his arms with the coat on had been pushed through the loops of the rope which cut tightly into his arms through the coat-sleeves. The time taken for the coat to be put on again was approximately five to six seconds.

Intermittently, light rain of real objective cold water fell on sitters' faces.

Finally, the table which stood slightly behind and to one side of the medium's chair, and in front of which two trumpets, both luminous, were standing, was levitated to the centre of the room without obscuring the view of the two luminous trumpets. The table would have to have been lifted over to have brought it there normally. The trumpets never moved. To have lifted the table normally from its original position to the middle of the room without knocking down or hiding the trumpets, it would have been necessary for a man to stand and lift it five or six feet in the air, over the heads of the seated sitters.

In two hours of physical phenomena there was not one thing that I did not eye with the critical scrutiny of a sceptical investigator—and not one thing failed to convince me that it was, and only could have been, wholly supernormal in its nature.

CHAPTER VII

REPORT OF A SÉANCE BY "CASSANDRA"
(*Daily Mirror*)

THE following report occupied the best part of the two centre pages of the *Daily Mirror* on February 28th, 1939. "Cassandra" is the pen-name of a gentleman on the staff of the *Daily Mirror* who writes a daily pertinent review on matters in general. He is well known for his cryptic and biting sarcasm, and has, on numbers of occasions, given full vent to his opposition to spiritualism.

The séance in question was held in North London at a place to which the medium had never been before, and the people present were complete strangers. Mr Leon Isaacs had been asked to take infra-red photographs. The problem arose as to the means of transporting the equipment, and since "Cassandra" had a car, he was asked to help this way. Thus the only reason why "Cassandra" was present was because he possessed a car.

The article was illustrated by a photograph (Plate No. 14), with the following description beneath it: "The medium in a trance, lashed to the chair, while a table leaves the ground and books fly through the air . . , a photograph taken during the séance attended by 'Cassandra'."

The heading was " 'Cassandra' got a surprise at Séance," and his report, in his caustic manner, reads as follows:

"I claim I can bring as much scepticism to bear on spiritualism as any newspaper writer living, and that's a powerful load of scepticism these days. I haven't got an open mind on the subject—I'm a violent, prejudiced unbeliever with a limitless ability to leer at the unknown. At least, I was till last

Saturday. And then I got a swift, sharp, ugly jolt that shook most of my pet sneers right out of their sockets.

"Picture to yourself a small room in a typical suburban house. In one corner a radio-gramophone. In the centre a ring of chairs. At the far end an armchair.

"About a dozen people filed in and sat in the circle. I hope they won't mind my saying it, but they struck me as a credulous collection that would have brought tears of joy to a share-pusher's eyes.

"Almost everyone a genuine customer for a lovely phony gold brick.

"They sat down and the medium, a young Welsh ex-miner, was then roped to the arm-chair. The photographer and I stood outside the circle. The lights went out and we sailed rapidly into the unknown.

"The medium gurgled like water running out of a bath, and we opened up with a strangled prayer.

"The circle of believers answered with 'All Hail the Power of Jesu's Name,' and I was told that we were 'on the brink.' I thought we were in Cockfosters, Herts, but I soon began to doubt it when trumpets sprayed with luminous paint shot round the room like fishes in a tank. They hovered like pike in a stream, and then swam slowly about.

"The medium snored and struggled for breath.

"Hymns, Trumpets.

"Somebody put a record on, and we were soon bellowing *'Daisy, Daisy, give me your answer, do.'*

The trumpets beat time and hurled themselves against the ceiling.

"A bell rang.

"There was considerable excited laughter, and in a slight hysteria we sang 'There is a green hill far away,' followed by the profane, secular virility of 'John Brown's body.'

"A tambourine with 'God is Love' written on it became highly unreasonable, and flew up noisily round our heads.

"The rough stertorious breathing of the medium continued, and a faint tapping sound heralded a voice speaking from one of the trumpets that was well adrift from its moorings. A faint, childish voice said in a voice of deep melancholy that it was 'Very, very happy.' More voices spoke.

"Water was splashed about (there was none in the room when we started) and books took off from their shelves.

"*Table moved.*

"The medium remained lashed to his chair.

"A clockwork train ran across the floor.

"Suddenly a heavy table slowly left the ground. The man who was sitting next to it said calmly: 'The table's gone!' The photographer released his flash—you see the result on the right.

"At no time did the medium move from his chair. I swear it.

"The table landed with a thump in the middle of the circle. A book that was on it remained in position.

"I'll pledge my word that not a soul in the room touched it. It was so heavy that it needed quite a husky fellow to lift it. I felt the weight of it afterward.

"What price cynicism ? What price heresy?

"Don't ask me what it all means, but you can't tell me now that these strange and rather terrifying things don't happen.

"I was there. I saw them. I went to scoff.

"But the laugh is sliding slowly round to the other side of my face.

"(Signed) 'CASSANDRA'."

CHAPTER VIII

THE REMOVAL AND REPLACING OF THE COAT

A FREQUENTLY performed phenomenal feat at séances is the removal and replacing of the medium's coat, while the medium is helplessly bound to his chair.

The preliminary preparation for this occurrence may vary in two ways.

A piece of thin cotton, the breaking strain of which is very slight, ties the top button of the coat to the buttonhole. Any slight strain on this cotton would snap it.

Alternatively, the two sides of the coat are sewn down the front, body-tight, extending from the revers of the coat to the skirt. Fancy stitching can be employed and the cotton knotted and tied round each button. Sometimes the coat has been sewn so high up to the neck that an aperture of only six inches diameter has been left.

The medium is then secured to the arm-chair as previously described.

Early in the séance, immediately after some of the other phenomena, such as the levitation of articles, the members of the circle sitting on either side of the medium are asked by the Guide to hold the medium's hands. Then, within one or two seconds, the coat is heard to fall as it is either thrown on the floor or on to a sitter's lap. Immediately after this there comes the request for "Light!" There is no delay whatsoever between the falling of the coat and light being switched on.

The light shows the roped medium's hands still held by the sitters. The coat is examined and there is not the slightest variation in the stitching. To conceive of the coat being unstitched, removed, and then re-stitched is a fantastic impossibility.

Plates Nos. 3 and 4 show the coat partially removed. It will be seen that while the head and shoulders are still within the coat the arms are outside the sleeves. In attempting to reproduce this condition normally, considerable bunching of the coat at the shoulders could not be avoided. In the photographs the entire absence of bunching should be noted. Several other factors should be taken into account when considering these pictures: firstly, that when the coat has been discarded, the roping on the medium's arms does not vary by the smallest fraction; secondly, the time factor between action and immediate light; and thirdly, there is no sound of movement during the coat's removal.

Plate No. 5 shows the coat entirely removed from the body and ready to be discarded. It will be noted in these photographs that the medium's hair is undisturbed, and this is invariable.

Plate No. 6 shows the coat discarded while the medium's hands are secured. (The gentleman holding the medium's hand is Mr Harold Sharp, the well-known medium in whose séance room the sitting took place.)

Plates Nos. 8 and 9 *[see p.74]* show the method whereby the coat is removed by dematerialization. The National Spiritualists Union badge can be seen in the lapel. If an article is left in the coat pocket, especially letters, these are found at the medium's feet when the coat has been removed, owing to the article not having been dematerialized. This photograph is more extensively dealt with in the chapter, "The Astral Head."

A report by Mr A.J. Case, President of the Cambridge Research Society, published in the *Psychic News* on August 12th, 1939, bears witness to the dematerialized condition of the coat in transit from and to the body.

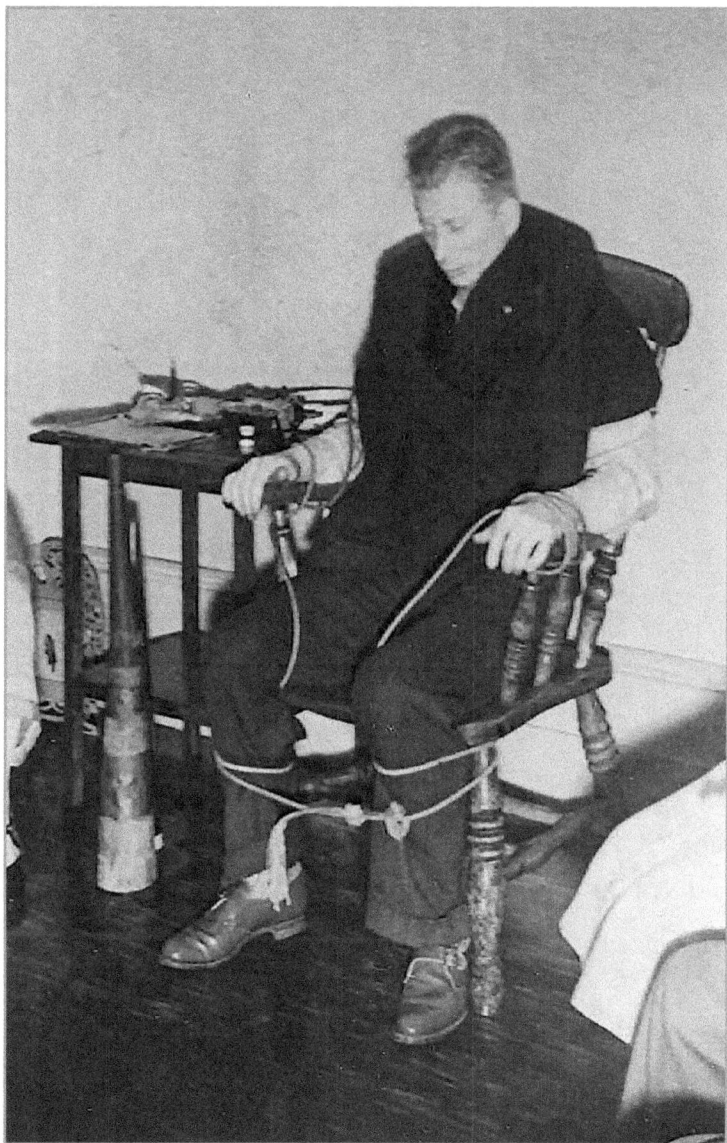

Leon Isaacs

PLATE 3. THE REMOVAL OF THE COAT

The medium is roped to the chair. His coat is sewn up. His head and body are still inside the coat, while the sleeves have been removed.

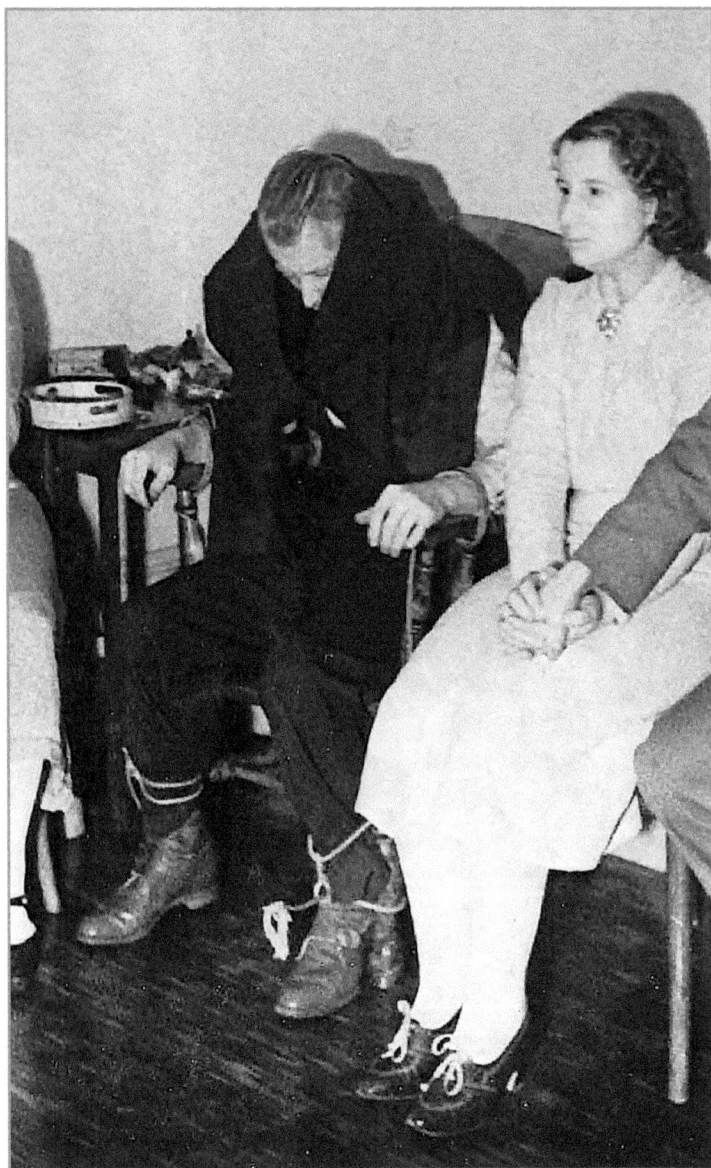

Leon Isaacs

PLATE 4. THE REMOVAL OF THE COAT

The coat-sleeves have been removed from the body and the coat is being drawn over the head.

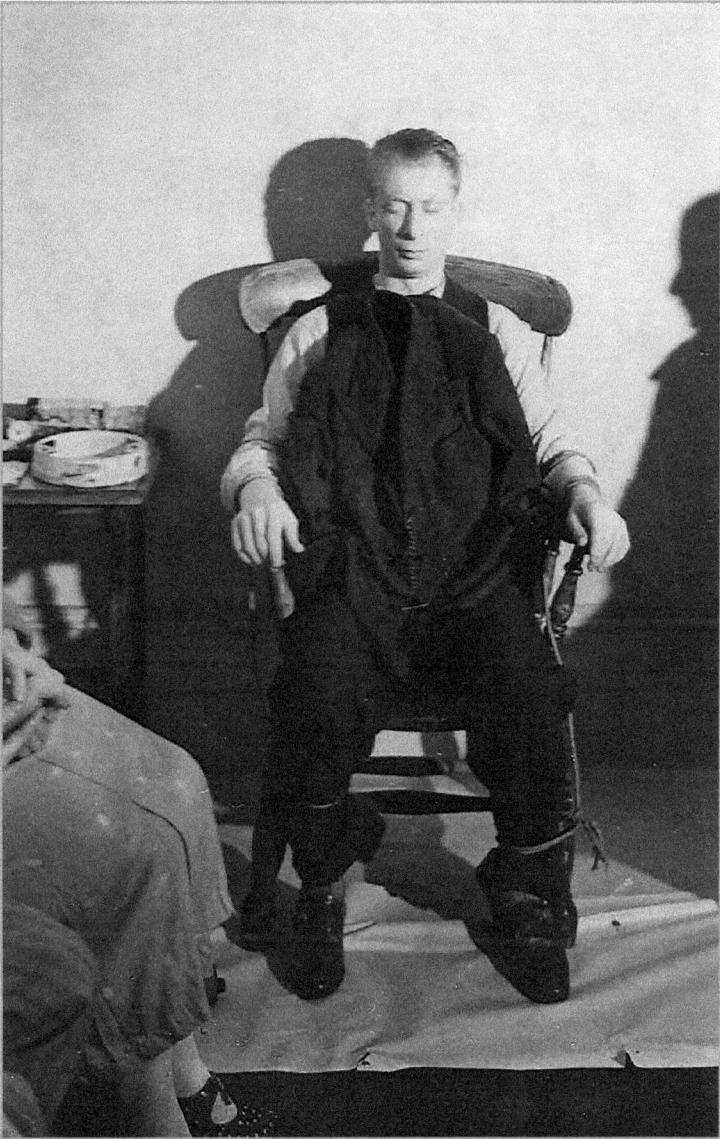

Daily Mirror Photographer

PLATE 5. THE REMOVAL OF THE COAT

The coat, entirely removed, is in front of the medium's body. Note the unruffled hair, the stitching of the coat and the roping of the medium's arms at the elbows.

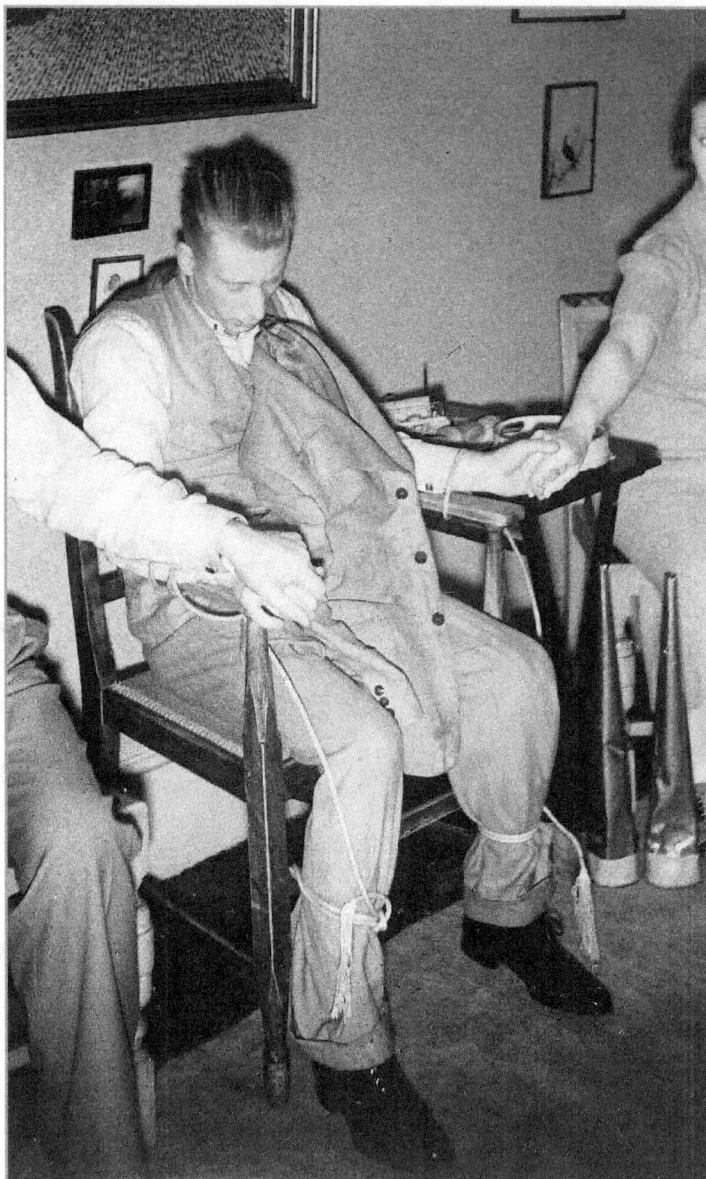

Leon Isaacs

PLATE 6. THE REMOVAL OF THE COAT
The coat removed from the body while the medium's hands are held.

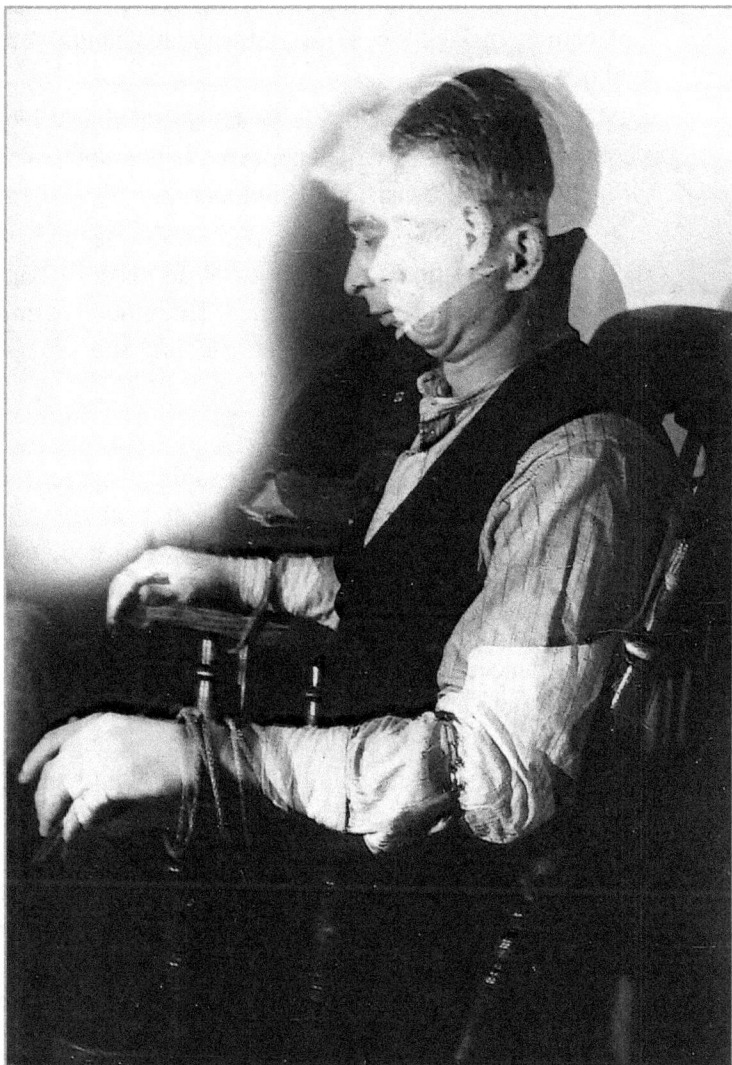

W. Clayton

PLATE 8. THE ASTRAL HEAD

The coat almost dematerialised. Note the badge on the coat-lapel [close to shirt collar]. The outer face is the astral head, the inner face being transfigured by the controlling Guide. The astral hands are also seen.

Mr Case writes:

> "One of the most baffling things was the removal and replacement of Jack Webber's coat while his hands were held on each side.
>
> While holding his hand, I felt a substance almost like a cobweb on my wrist, which appeared to get more solid till it assumed the consistency of cloth.
>
> It seemed to have no weight. After a few seconds it slid gently to the floor. The light went up instantly, and there sat the medium minus his coat. Both the coat and the ropes were examined and the stitches and knots found intact as before."

The Dean of Trinity College afterwards said "wherever the power came from he was quite satisfied that trickery was impossible." Prince Deo and his friend, who had had considerable experience of the occult in India, said that "fraud was out of the question." (*Psychic News*, August 12th, 1939.)

The coat is placed on the floor somewhere near to the medium (within six to eight feet). The Guide will again ask two sitters to hold the medium's hands, then says he is going to try to replace the coat. The sitters holding the hands often feel the coat, free of the body, being lifted up preparatory to its replacement. Within a very few seconds comes the call for light when the coat is seen back on the medium's body under the ropes. The stitching and roping are again examined, and they are found to be precisely the same as originally tied. The time factor is again important—as a rule five seconds only between the coat being felt free of the body, and the light showing its replacement.

There are two items that should be mentioned. The first is that during the time the coat has been off the body, the arms have swelled so that the ropes are pressing tightly into the flesh. The author, has, with others, been asked to note the tightness and has tried to move the ropes a fraction, but so tight have they been that any movement of them was not possible. To insert a coat-sleeve under the ropes was almost an impossibility and could only have been normally achieved after a very long struggle—if it were possible at all. Secondly, when the coat has been returned under these very tight ropes, there is not any rocking or bunching of the sleeves.

The chapter on "The Securing of the Medium" deals with this phenomenon, when cotton was tied and knotted round the medium's coat-cuff buttons.

The first time this phenomenon was photographed (the technique of holding the medium's hands has been developed since) Mr Maurice Barbanell, the Editor of the *Psychic News*, was present, and in reporting the incident he wrote:

"These photographs are a challenge to materialistic science, for they demonstrate what is regarded as the 'impossible'.

The removal of a coat through ropes—this means that either the coat or the ropes dematerialized to allow matter to pass through matter . . . proves the existence of a psychic law which materialists refuse to accept.

Jack Webber, a 'physical medium', was securely roped to his chair, the knots being threaded with black cotton which normally would snap if interfered with.

Black cotton was also tied around a button and knotted through a button-hole of his jacket, so that the slightest movement on his part would have broken them. Yet all these knots and threads were intact at the end of the séance.

The removal of the coat and its reappearance in its original position could not have been done by the medium. None of the sitters was responsible, as they were all controlled, everybody linking hands with his neighbours.

The feat was accomplished by an invisible intelligence. Whose was it ?

Conjuring is out of the question. No magician could have emulated this happening, under the same conditions, nor at the speed with which it was accomplished—three seconds for the coat's removal, and six seconds for its replacement.

Fraud is out of the question."

The following extracts are taken from an article published in *Light* (page 427-428, 1939), written by Mr B. Abdy Collins, C.I.E., well known for his books and writings on psychical research.

". . . I wish to draw attention to one phenomenon which is quite in a class by itself and cannot be explained; they are explained by those who accept the facts, as caused by psychic rods or voice boxes emanating from the medium and directed by his sub-conscious mind.

The phenomenon to which I refer is the removal and replacement of Mr Webber's coat. In order that its importance may be clearly appreciated, I will briefly describe what happens. Mr Webber wears an ordinary closely fitting black lounge coat, which is sewn up all down the front with a needle and coarse thread by one of the sitters. He then sits in an armchair into which he is securely bound. The middle of a long piece of rope is fastened to the back of the chair and Mr Webber's arms are tightly tied to the arms and his legs to the legs of the chair. This is effected by two sitters each taking one end of the rope and winding it round and round his limbs and the chair arm and leg, securing it with knots here and there and finally bringing the ends of the rope together, when they are sewn up and sealed in several places . . .

The two persons sitting either side of him are then asked each to grasp one of his hands. 'Black Cloud', the s*oi-disant* Guide, speaking through the medium, then announces that the coat will be removed, and the light is switched off. In a very short while, he again asks for the light to be turned on, and there is Mr Webber sitting bound in his chair as before, but his coat has been removed with the stitches in front intact. It may be lying on the medium's knees or on the lap of one of the sitters. After any examination the sitters wish, 'Black Cloud' announces that he will replace the coat, the two sitters grasp the medium's hands and the light is switched off. Very soon, 'Black Cloud' calls for light and Mr Webber is found sitting in the chair, his hands still held, and the coat on him again as it was at first.

The facts are undoubted. They have been 'witnessed', if that is the proper word, by many hundreds of persons. I myself have twice 'seen' the coat removed in this way and once 'seen' it replaced. The coat is removed while Mr Webber's hands are held, his arms are tightly bound to the arms of the chair and the front of the coat is closely stitched together. It is not a conjuring trick. How is it done?

The only explanation seems to be that the coat is 'dematerialized' in some way, or else that matter as represented by the coat is passed through matter as represented by Mr Webber. Anyway, this is a phenomenon which cannot be explained by invisible psychic rods, or 'pseudo-pods'. Apports brought into a closed room have been explained in much the same way as I have suggested, but our sceptics get over this simply by denying that any case of an apport is properly substantiated. Here they cannot deny the facts.

If they refuse to accept the testimony of others, they can easily verify the facts themselves. What 'explanation' can they offer.

If nothing will induce them to accept the spiritist hypothesis, then at least they must admit that some unknown force does somehow remove the coat. The scientific world will at last have to agree that there are phenomena which are not governed by physical laws, and that there is something beyond the material world, as hitherto unknown. For myself, it seems less absurd to ascribe these activities to 'spirits' than to try to explain them by the activities of the medium's subconscious mind. The latter hypothesis seems to get us nowhere. It does not explain how the coat is removed and replaced. We require an intelligence with a knowledge and ability that is more than human. . . "

This phenomenon is also testified to in other descriptions of séances.

ADDENDUM, MARCH 1940

Plate No. 7. This photograph was obtained on February 28th, twelve days before the passing of Mr Webber, and was the last secured.

The first photographs secured dealt with the coat phenomenon, and the last deals with the same subject, providing a mystery-picture that can only be described as "impossible."

For some months, work in the developing circle had been directed towards the manifesting of materialized forms in red light and the removal of the coat and the more general forms of the physical phenomena had not been encouraged. No other apparatus was brought into the circle except the trumpet and the luminous plaques.

The coat was not sewn up, and had not been interfered with for a considerable time. Roping was always employed.

During the sitting came the request for photograph, and after the exposure was made the Guide said it would show the coat with the sleeves under the ropes, while other parts of the coat had been "removed."

The photograph shows a position that it is impossible to reproduce, even normally, with one coat. The members of the circle have spent some time trying to reproduce normally what

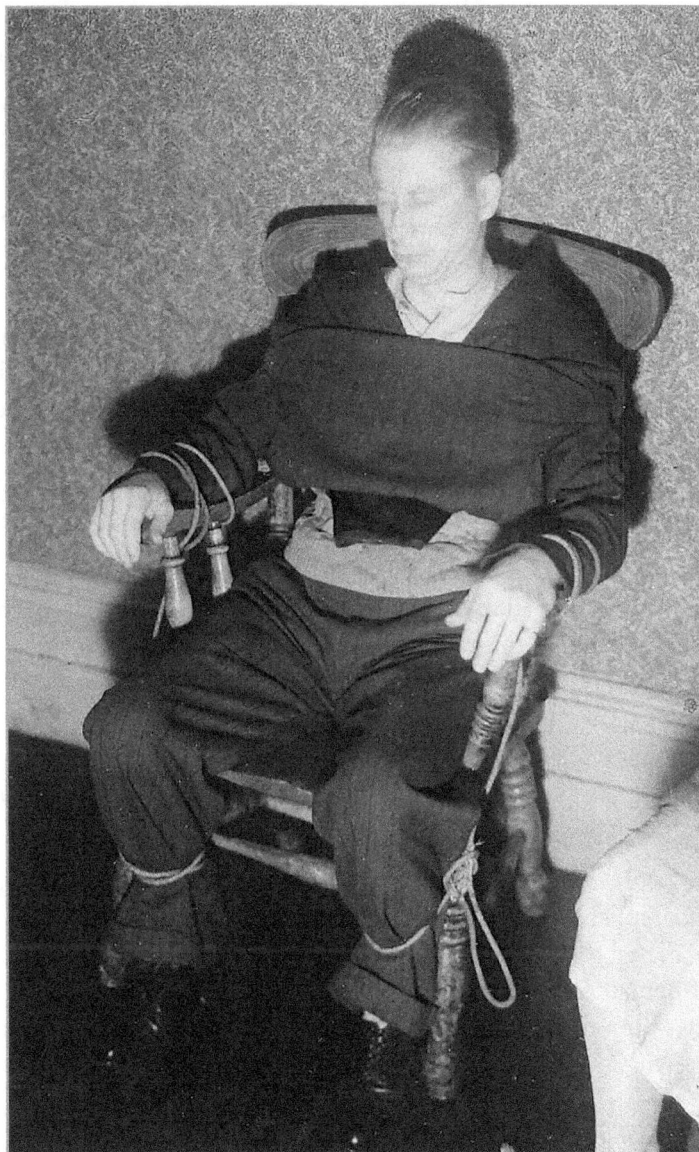

Harry Edwards

PLATE 7. THE REMOVAL OF THE COAT

The last photograph secured through Webber's mediumship shows the back of his coat in front of his body, while the sleeves are on the arms under the ropes. It is normally impossible to reproduce this effect.

the photograph shows, and a general invitation is extended to the public to reproduce it.

Examination of the photograph under magnification shows that the pattern and texture of the coat is identical throughout.

It will be observed that the coat-sleeves are on the arms under the ropes, the shoulders and lapels of the coat are in their proper position, but the back of the coat is draped across the front of the body.

The author affirms most definitely that Mr Webber had only one suit of this pattern, that only one coat was present at the séance, and that it was impossible for a second coat of such precise pattern and texture to have been in the room.

Before the author had time to change the plates and light bulb, there came a request for a second photograph. As the apparatus was not ready, this was lost.

Immediately after this the coat fell to the floor, the white light was put on, and the coat was examined. It was quite normal.

The only possible way in which the position depicted in this remarkable photograph can be normally reproduced is with two coats or extra material. With two coats there is so much bunching that a reproduction becomes a caricature of the photograph.

There is one logical explanation of how this feat was accomplished. For the coat to be shown as photographed it must be in two parts, and the suggestion is made that using the process of dematerialization the Guide separated the back part of the coat from the collar downwards, and reformed it in the position shown.

When discussing the photograph with Mr Webber, he put forward the thesis that the back part of the coat was first dematerialized and brought through the body (as an apport is produced through the body) and rematerialized in front of him.

While no one can speak with authority as to the precise method employed by the Guide, the author suggests that the former thesis is supported by the piece of cloth hanging down below the abdomen, which may be the top part of the back of the coat where it joins the collar, especially as in this portion the lining and a seam, consistent with this theory, is shown.

In the attempts to reproduce normally this position, a second person to drape the coat was essential, and the experiment occupied some considerable space of time, with attendant noise. For the medium to reproduce normally the position from a roped condition and to return to a roped condition would be absolutely impossible.

If trickery is contemplated, all the persons present must have been implicated, since collusion would be impossible without the knowledge of all sitters. In a subsequent photograph taken later at the end of the sitting, the roping was portrayed precisely, even to the crossing of the ropes, etc., as shown in this picture.

Thus we are faced with a photograph of a position, impossible to reproduce, that must have required supernormal powers beyond human capacity.

CHAPTER IX

THE PROCESS OF APPORTING OBJECTS

ON only one occasion has the process of apporting objects been photographed.

Only on rare occasions have objects been apported through Mr Webber's mediumship. The following is the narrative of events that led to the securing of the photographs referred to.

The occasion was a public sitting, at which about eight members of the Temple of Truth, Paddington, were present, on November 8th, 1938. The following quoted description was signed as an accurate description of the incident by Mr James Sing, President, of the Temple of Truth.

REPORT OF INCIDENT AT SITTING WITH MR JACK WEBBER
ON NOVEMBER 8TH 1938

Conversation between Paddy, the child control, and the Chairman, Harry Edwards :

PADDY. "I would like to bring something into this room to show we can bring objects through walls and doors."

CH. "We should be glad if you will try to do this."

PADDY. "I will go and see what I can find."

(A few minutes later)

PADDY. "In the next room is a bird with long legs."

CH. "Yes, I know, it is a bird called a crane and is made of brass.

PADDY. "I will try and bring it. It has to come through the medium's body."

(A few minutes later—a camera was ready to take photograph.)

GUIDE (BLACK CLOUD). "Take photograph."

(As this was done an object fell to the floor.)

GUIDE. "Put on the light."

(When this was done the brass bird was found to have been brought from the next room and was on the floor.)

GUIDE. "If the photograph has been taken correctly, it will show the bird passing from the body of the medium in ectoplasm."

All windows and doors were locked and never opened.

Signed as an accurate description of the incident.

JAMES SING,

President,

Temple of Truth, Paddington.

Three photographs are printed (Plate Nos. 10,11 and 12). No. 10 shows the whole of the picture as taken. The bird and ectoplasm can be seen near the medium's solar plexus. No. 11 is an enlargement of the area concerned. In No. 12a is a picture of the apported bird.

It will be noted that this event was produced in accordance with a plan stated beforehand. First, by Paddy, who told the sitters what was intended, and who was seconded by Black Cloud who foretold what would be on the photographic plate before it was developed. Here is signal evidence of extraneous intelligences operating laws unknown to human beings.

The brass ornament is three and three-quarters of an inch high and weighs two ounces. This object was definitely passed through the wall and/or door of one room into another. To achieve this, the ornament must have been rendered into a

68

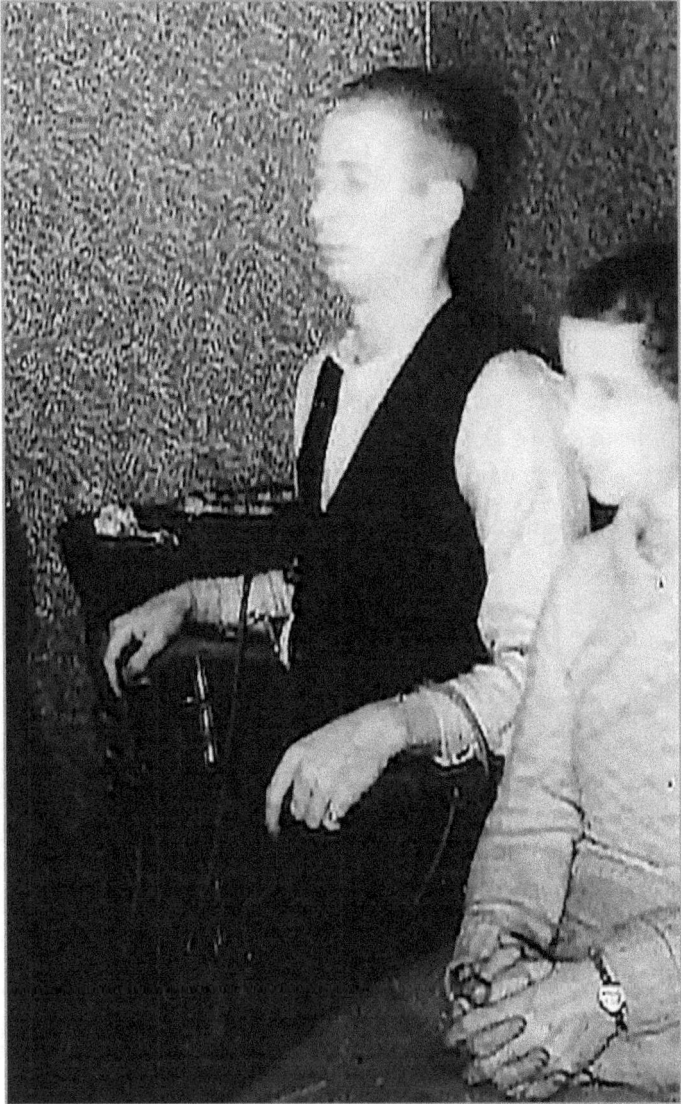

J. McCulloch

PLATE 10. THE PROCESS OF APPORTING

The photograph with sitters cropped. Note the apport appearing by the right arm. See photograph opposite for detail of apported bird.

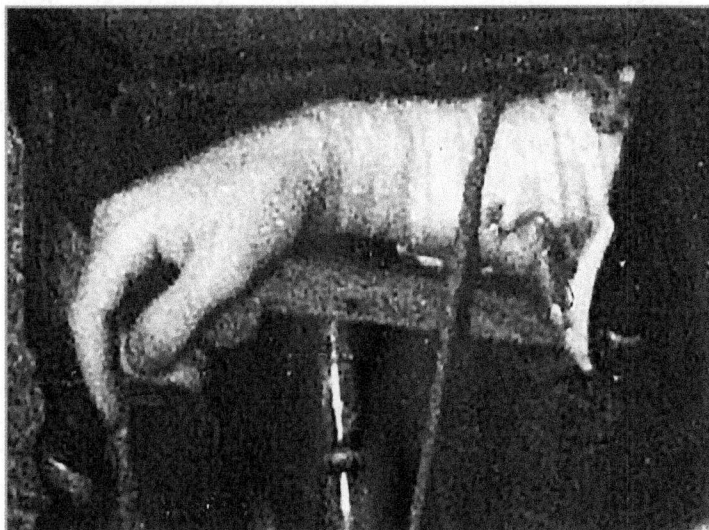

J. McCulloch

PLATE 11. THE PROCESS OF APPORTING

An enlargement of a section of Plate 10. The brass bird with ectoplasm is seen emerging from the medium's body. This is the first photograph showing the act of apporting.

Left: PLATE 12a. *Detail of apported brass bird.(Extracted from Plate 12)*

dematerialized condition of a vibration so high that it would pass through solid obstacles as sound passes through a brick wall. In this condition it passed through the medium's body and rematerialized on emerging. The ectoplasmic state at the emerging doubtless is an essential factor for the rematerialization, as is necessary for all forms of materializations.

This process, demonstrating that apported objects have to come via the medium's body, is consistent with the usual procedure of apport mediums, who are able to produce apports, using a trumpet for their delivery.[1]

The trumpet is connected to the medium by an ectoplasmic arm as in Plate No.19 [p.93]. The apport in its dematerialized condition travels via the medium's body along the ectoplasmic arm into the mouth of the trumpet, where it is materialized ; the trumpet acting as a conserver or retainer for the ectoplasmic force and the act of materialization.

On a later occasion the apporting of two objects was witnessed in red light. For some hours before a séance when apports may occur, Mr Webber feels a tightness of the abdomen and is therefore able, at times, to know what is intended. On the occasion referred to, he had these symptoms, and therefore he invited a search to be made of his person, which was carried out by a member of the circle (Mr S. Croft), a member of the Metropolitan Police Force, in the séance room before all the sitters, just previous to his sitting down for roping.

1. The method of apporting objects via the medium's body is not applicable to all apport mediums. The author was present in April 1940, at a sitting with another medium, where apports were received by a different process. On this occasion the trumpet, previously shown to be empty, was taken to the ceiling, to receive the apport (in this case a glass vase). The explanation from the Guide is that the object is transformed into a vibratory state and contained in an etheric envelope. The object is then rematerialized within the trumpet. Another apport produced on this occasion was a finely engraved seal, which rematerialized while the trumpet was describing circular movements of amazing speed—at first faint tappings could be heard in the rapidly moving trumpet, gradually becoming stronger as the materializing process was completed.

He did not leave the presence of the sitters, but immediately sat down for roping. The red light was on, sufficiently bright for all to see the medium with his arms bound to the chair. Trumpets were in levitation—also clearly discernible in the red light—one of these turned round, presenting its large opening to the solar plexus region and an object was heard to fall into it.

It then came to the author who was asked to take out of the trumpet the article within—an Egyptian ornament. (See Plate No.12). After a minute or two the trumpet again travelled to the solar plexus and another object was heard to fall into it. This, too, was taken out of the trumpet by the sitter to whom it was presented (Mr S. Croft). See Plate No. 12 in this case, a stone Buddha. It will be seen from the photographs that the size of the objects could not have been hidden from an experienced searcher. Furthermore, all the eleven persons present saw the medium tied to the chair and the trumpet which had a second before been in very violent levitation move to the medium's body, when the article was heard to fall into the trumpet. Ectoplasm was not seen at the time of emergence of these two objects. This is easily understood since the process was being executed in red light and ectoplasm is in its strongest form or highest vibration when invisible.

Plate No.12 also shows an apport produced the week previous to the above incident, but this was produced in darkness, and pinned directly on the lady's dress, to whom it was given (Mrs G. Layton).

At séances elsewhere, apports are occasionally produced. On one occasion a coin commemorating the year 1915 in an American State. The recipient (Mr Gordon Grahame) said he had been in that State in that particular year: At the same séance, a lady received a crucifix that she had been informed, by another medium, would be given to her.

It is a pertinent fact that Mr Webber gave this sitting at a few hours' notice. He and the author were invited to attend a sitting with another medium at Luton when this medium wired that he could not be present owing to illness. The organizer, Mr Gordon Grahame, telephoned Mr Webber to ask if he would sit, so that on this occasion there could not have been any preconceived action on Mr Webber's part, and the lady who received the crucifix came from Bedford—a complete stranger both to Mr Grahame and to Mr Webber.

PLATE 12. APPORTS[2]

All these objects were apported at Webber séances including the brass bird shown on p69. Here are shown a stone Buddha, a Mosaic ornament and an Egyptian ornament of Osiris.

---

2. The original plate of Apports contained the Brass bird also, but for ease of viewing it was decided to divide the photographic plate as shown. (Publisher)

CHAPTER X

THE ASTRAL HEAD

THIS photograph is one of the most remarkable yet secured, for here has been photographed for the first time, and physically, an astral or spirit head.

The photographer (Mr W.J. Clayton) was not a spiritualist, and the only reason he was present at the séance was that he possessed a camera. This camera was of the box type and fixed to an ordinary though somewhat rickety tripod.

This photograph is so important that consideration is given to the possibility of error on the part of the photographer or complicity on the part of the medium.

The question of a double exposure is ruled out by the precision of the sitters as well as the body of the medium. It should be borne in mind that a period of several minutes, with the white light on, occurred between each exposure (the flash bulb had to be changed and plates withdrawn, and new plates inserted). The rickety state of the photographer's stand was also an item that would have prevented such precision if it had been a double photograph. It is not credible that a sitter could so precisely retain or resume a posture so photographically exact.

The photograph was taken at an exposure speed of one-fiftieth of a second, by sashalite flash. Knowledge of the number of exposures made and the recording on the other plates in the camera, prevents the theory of double exposure remaining tenable.

If it were possible for the medium to register these two distinct impressions, he would have to have done so within a

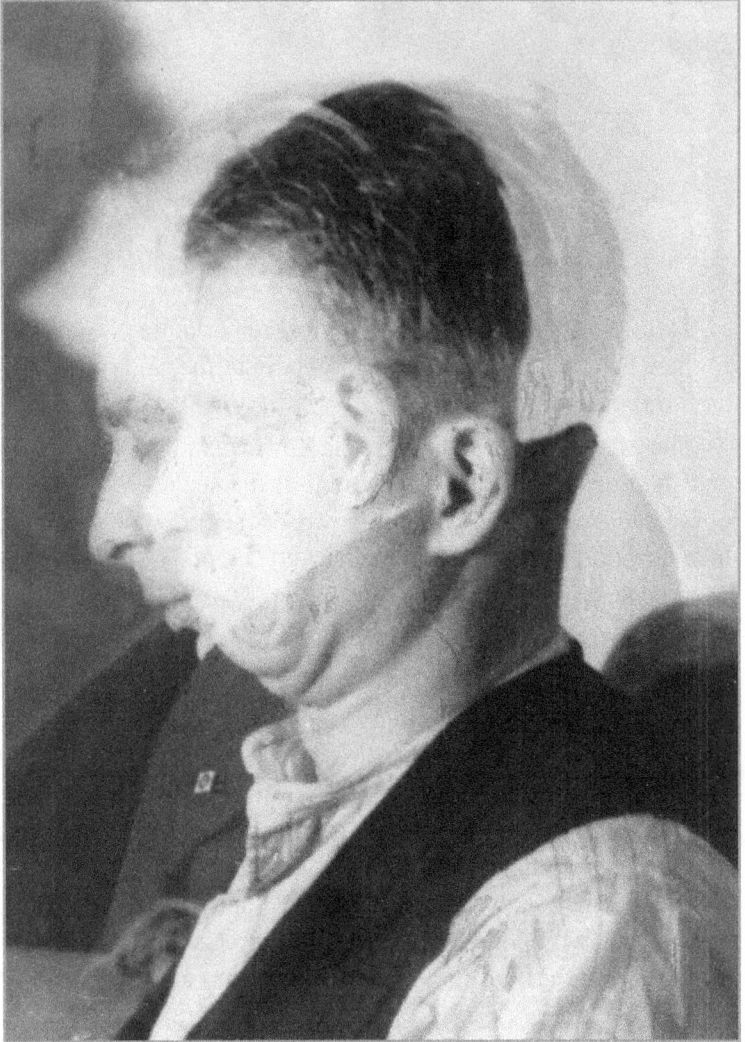

W. Clayton

PLATE 9. THE ASTRAL HEAD

An enlargement of the head in Plate 8. The double density in the centre is where the two heads merge. No fully physical head was in existence at the time of the photographic exposure.

fraction of the fiftieth of a second exposure without movement, leaving each image to register precisely on the plate. Also he would have had to have judged the changing of his expression to coincide with the precise fiftieth part of a second during which the flash occurred—an obviously impossible feat. Thus, there can be no other conclusion than that the two faces were in physical being simultaneously during the exposure.

The Guide has said that the outer face is "the spirit face."

It is impossible to suggest any other reasoned statement as to what the outer face can be, and it therefore remains that this must be the astral or spirit counterpart of the medium. Further examination of the photograph supports this view.

The inner face is not Mr Webber's normal face but shows a transfiguration by the Guide, a tenable thesis when the astral body is outside the physical body and the Guide is in control.

The outer face is a perfect face, devoid of expression. It should be noted how the chin of the astral face stops short where it meets the lapel of the coat, showing the harmony of density between the dematerialized coat and the astral face.

The alignment of the two faces is precise, but whilst it can be seen that the eyes and mouth are in line, the ears are not, which indicates that a rotary motion is necessary for one head to join the other. This rotary movement provides evidence that the two heads are three dimensional, that is, it is not one face superimposed over the other, and is further evidence that the picture is not the result of a double exposure.

There is not a physical head in existence.

The rear part of the inner head is in a state of partial dematerialization, as is seen by its transparency. The darker part within the two heads is where the two heads merge, bringing the total density of the two heads to normality.

The astral head possesses breadth, as evidenced where the strand of hair on the astral head is shown over the hair of the inner head. This may be more readily understood if the rotary motion of the merging of one head over the other is taken into account.

This photograph was obtained primarily in order to illustrate the dematerialized condition of the coat when being removed or restored to the medium's body. (See Chapter 8: "The Removal and Replacing of the Coat.")

It provides proof of the thesis held by spiritualists that each person possesses, while in the physical condition, an astral body, which leaves the flesh at the time of the physical death, to continue in a "spirit" sphere of activity.

Since this photograph was taken, there have been further incidents in Mr Webber's developing circle that bear out the ability of the Guides to dematerialize the physical body. The first incident occurred in a good red light, when the medium's head, hands, and arms were seen to have vanished. The sitters nearby were able to look down into the cavity formed by the neck part of the clothing and only a black void was to be observed.

Mrs Webber, who sat near to the medium on this occasion, was rather alarmed at the condition of the medium.

On a subsequent evening, in a duller red light, one not sufficient to see the medium as clearly as on the above occasion, the Rev. Maurice Elliott and Mr Byerley of *The Link*, who were present, were invited by the Guide to feel the space where the medium's hands and arms should be roped to the chair. They were not there, and the Rev. Maurice Elliott slid his hand up inside one of the medium's coat-sleeves but could feel no arm there. Then the medium's hands and arms returned almost instantaneously.

This chapter is a recital of facts without elaboration; much could be written upon the implications of this photograph, and the importance of being able to provide a physical photograph of the spirit body.

CHAPTER XI

LEVIATION OF THE MEDIUM

PART of the demonstration of psychic power given at séances is the levitation of the medium—who is throughout bound to his chair—from the place where he is sitting to another part of the room or hall.

Several attempts have been made to photograph this phenomenon, but without evidential success.

The process involves the lifting up of the medium with his chair into the air, where he often stays for a number of minutes, and then depositing him in a place as far from his original position as the room or hall allows.

At times during such levitation the medium's feet are felt travelling round on the heads of the sitters. When there has been some light present, such as a luminous spot on the wall or perhaps where there has been a dull emergence of light through a curtain, the body in the chair has been seen in suspension. On occasions in halls where the roof is high, not only is it clear from the sound of the voice that the medium is high up, but evidence is provided of the levitation by the movement of light fittings that could only be reached with a ladder.

Further, when the table has been previously levitated out into the room, the medium is deposited with only the smallest margin of room between the table and the sitters to spare.

This phenomenon usually takes place at the end of the séance when the floor space before the medium is occupied with luminous trumpets and other objects, to wriggle the chair and himself from one position to another.

The following is an extract from a letter dealing with the levitation of the medium, published in the *Two Worlds*, February 24th, 1939, by Mr J.W. Byerley, Chairman of *The Link* :

". . . Twenty-four sitters were around the walls; white light on; Webber securely bound in his chair; three-foot-six-inch table obliquely across centre of circle, leaving only a narrow gangway between sitters; luminous trumpet on floor at sitters' feet, half-right inclined to me. Lights put out—my eyes were on the trumpet. If the medium passed between my eye-level and the floor, it would blot out the trumpet. He did not pass; no sound of medium moving (I was sitting next but one). Control's voice heard from ceiling; well to my left a gentle bump on the floor. Light put on—medium still tightly roped.

Admittedly it is possible for the medium to wriggle across the circle whilst bound in his chair, but to do this under the prevailing conditions, he would have to come forward two feet, turn to the right three or four feet, and then pass between the table and the sitters, which could not be done without bumping the table or sitters, and there was no sound of a moving chair. The total distance he would have to cover would be fifteen feet, an absolute impossibility in a few seconds without noise . . ."

Quite often marks from the medium's hair (from the hair preparation he uses) are seen upon the ceiling.

Plate No.13 illustrates an unusual happening. An attempt had been made to photograph the levitation, when by some means the power necessary to lift the medium was reversed. The sound of the chair coming down was heard, and then a continued grinding and cracking of considerable volume. When the light was put on, the medium was found tied to the wreckage of the chair.

Leon Isaacs

PLATE 13. THE BREAKING OF A CHAIR

The downward force completely breaks a substantial Windsor arm-chair. The seat was broken clearly across in two places. Legs, arms and struts were also broken.

The Windsor chair that he occupied was very strongly constructed. The seat was one and a quarter inches thick and this was broken right across in two places while the chair legs were forced out, as were the stays, and the arm-rest was broken away from the back. The photograph taken at the moment of breaking up clearly shows what is occurring. Please note the entire absence of strain or tension in the medium's body.

It is worthwhile to consider the amount of force necessary to break up a chair so completely. It is doubtful whether a very strong man could, by lifting and then smashing the chair down, break it as described. Remember the medium (as photographed at the moment of the smashing up of the chair) is in a roped condition, precluding, of course, any such collusion. This photograph is indicative of the tremendous forces brought into being by the spirit operators.

ADDENDUM, MARCH 1940.

On February 26th, at a séance given at the International Institute for Psychic Investigation, levitation took place. In descending, one of the rear legs of the arm-chair into which the medium was bound, was placed through a cross-stay of the table, which had previously been levitated to the far side of the circle—another impossible human feat, in total darkness, without noise, and definitely proving that the medium in his chair had been suspended in the air.

CHAPTER XII

TABLE LEVIATION

THESE photographs show tables in levitation. In each case the tables are well in front of the medium, though owing to the head-on focus they appear to be nearer to the medium than they actually are.

The table in Plate No. 14 weighs over 45 lb., and was very highly polished. "Cassandra" refers to this incident in his description of the seance as requiring a "husky" man to lift it. If this table was resting on the cushion, it would show indentation marks.

Comparison of the cushion on which the medium is seated, with that in Plate No.18 *[p.90]*, shows that the cushion is depressed. This record testifies to the theory of Professor Crawford that the weight levitated is returned through the medium.

Plate No.15 shows the table in levitation in front of Mr Bernard Gray of the *Sunday Pictorial* (the reason why Mr Gray is seen crouching is that the table a moment before had been dancing on his head and shoulders).

On other occasions while the table is levitated high in the air, a trumpet also rises and hits the table all round, to demonstrate that the table is indeed floating in the air.

ADDENDUM, MARCH 1940

On February 19th, 1940, at the International Institute for Psychic Investigation the table was levitated, circled round, and touched the heads of sitters, and finally descended with such force as to break the leg of the table completely off.

Leon Isaacs

PLATE 14. TABLE LEVITATION

The levitation of a table weighing over 45lbs. It is actually suspended supernormally in mid-air.

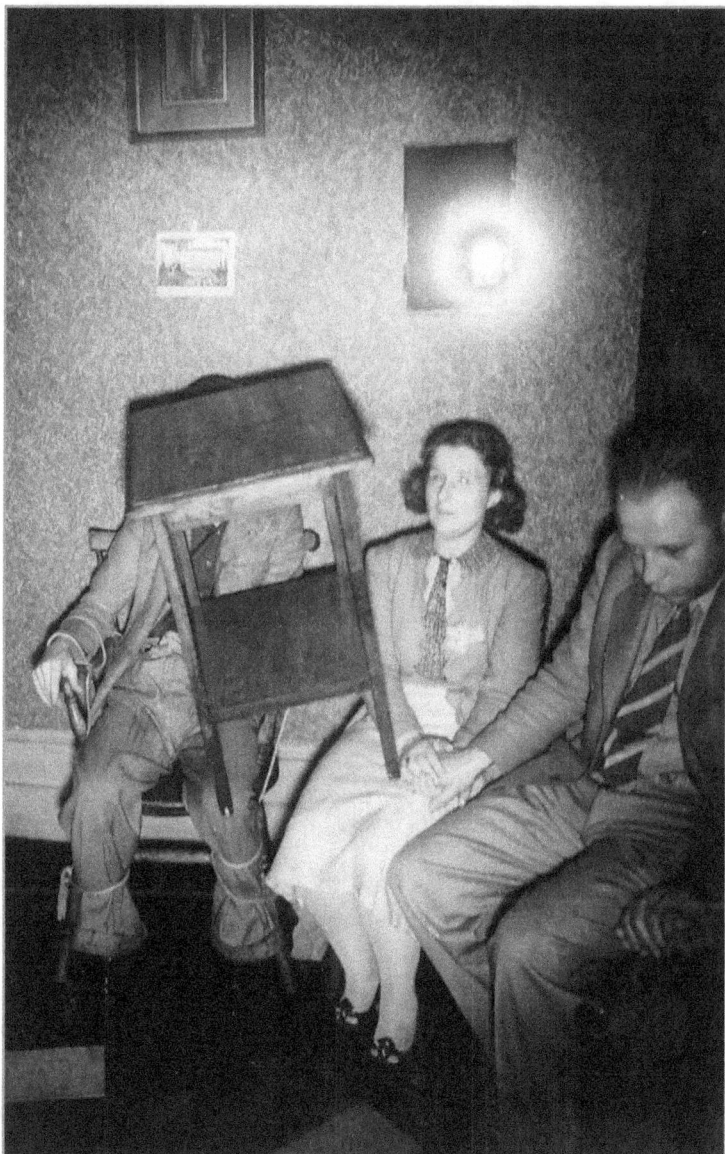

Leon Isaacs

PLATE 15. TABLE LEVITATION
The levitation of a table in the presence of Mr Bernard Gray, a
"Sunday Pictorial" investigator.

CHAPTER XIII

TRUMPET PHENOMENA

MR COLIN EVANS describes in his report, with some detail, trumpet movements.

The Guides have now brought their technique between trumpet movements and light to a perfect state. If the one who operates the white light responds immediately the call for light comes, the trumpets are seen in movement as the light goes on, these being well away from the medium helplessly bound in his chair. As the light is put out the trumpets ascend at once. They are often lying on the floor, yet this makes no difference, since they rise with force as soon as the room is darkened.

Four trumpets have been seen in simultaneous levitation. The best trumpet movement is with two trumpets. One may be at one end of the room and the other at the further end. One trumpet may be in the air knocking on the ceiling, while the other sweeps the floor. Tall people are unable either to hold up a trumpet so high as is accomplished in the séance or with both arms extended span the distance between the trumpets. May it again be stressed that, for such a movement to take place within a split second of light being put on, with the medium still entranced, bound in sealed ropes, with knots fastened with gummed tape or wax, provides incontrovertible evidence of spirit power.

In the red light, these movements are still more interesting, for the trumpets are then clearly seen to be floating about the room without visible means of control. Trumpets in levitation will move as requested by the sitters, turning completely round as if on an axis, first with the narrow end towards the medium, then with the broad end, and so on.

The trumpet will weave its way round the heads of the sitters, going past one side of the head with the broad end outwards, turning round the back of the head and coming back with the small end foremost, going to the next sitter in similar manner, and so on round the circle.

The speed at which the trumpets travel is phenomenal, so rapid that the luminous bases appear as a continuous band of light. At times they travel so fast that the eye cannot follow the movement even in the restricted area of a room.

To see two trumpets, moving at such a speed, weaving intricate patterns one with the other without ever hitting each other, provides an amazing spectacle.

It is often the case that there is an electric light pendant or a length of flex hanging from the ceiling in the centre of this trumpet activity. Only once has the electric fitting been smashed or the flex pulled down, though the trumpets in fast movement will suddenly slow up and gently touch the pendant.

Again the rapid movement may bring the trumpet to within a fraction of an inch of a sitter's nose, so that the wind caused by the movement is heard and felt.

Repeatedly the trumpet will do this in front of a sitter, then flash away to caress gently the face of another sitter on the opposite side of the room. The control of the trumpet is perfect.

For any person normally to execute such movements in total darkness without hitting a sitter or a hanging object would be an obvious impossibility.

To exhibit such controlled movement considerable energy must be present. This is evidenced by the marks that are made on the floor or linoleum when the trumpet sweeps the floor in large arcs.

Plate No. 16 (the trumpet has been outlined) shows the trumpet in movement close to a sitter; so rapid was the movement that the flash of the bulb was not fast enough to enable a precise trumpet to be photographed. On this occasion, the press switch to flash the exposure was tied to the arm of the medium's chair, and the Guide, through the medium, is pressing the switch with a finger, thus taking the photograph.

One phase of this phenomena that often causes apprehension on the part of a sitter is that the trumpet returns with great force, hitting the medium on his head. The Guide explains this as the return of a psychic rod, carrying the trumpet back with it to the medium.

On other occasions, for reasons not yet known, the medium has been unmercilessly beaten on the head with the trumpet continuously for some moments, the trumpet swinging with tremendous force and crashing down on the head. At one time a long heavy trumpet made of stout tin was in use and this would beat the medium's head. If a person were normal, surely he would soon be beaten into unconsciousness.

So terribly severe have been these beatings that the author could not believe, in the beginning, that the trumpets could have hit the head so hard—he believed they must have been hitting the wall. After the sitting, the wall was examined and there was not even the smallest indentation of the wallpaper.

At the next sitting the author was invited to place his hand sideways on the medium's head, while the trumpet crashed down upon it, to demonstrate that the trumpet did come in contact with the head.

After such events, it is particularly noteworthy that there is neither bruise nor bump on the medium's head, nor even the slightest red mark. The condition of his body in trance must not only be impervious to physical blows, etc., but the tissues must be "conditioned" not to re-act to blows, etc. A dead body will bruise . . . and it is still another mystery of the spirit people, how they are able so to protect a body from ill.

In this connection it is interesting to note that medical men who have been invited to take the medium's pulse while in

Leon Isaacs

PLATE 16. TRUMPET PHENOMENA

*The trumpet was moving so rapidly that in a 75th-second
exposure a precise image was not secured. The trumpet has
been inked in.*

trance, have declared it to be between 90 and 100—an appreciable acceleration. One doctor gave the opinion that it would be likely to prove fatal for such a pulse rate to be maintained for two hours, which is the usual duration of a séance.

The respirations have also been taken, and found to be nearly double the normal rate.

When a two-piece trumpet has been used, it has sometimes become separated, the two ends being widely apart. At one time, one end was outside the circle behind the sitters. This end was brought up behind the sitter, passed over the head and reunited with the other end. This separation and joining together has been observed on a number of occasions.

PLATE 17. TRUMPET PHENOMENA

The trumpet held to mouth by an ectoplasmic arm.

Leon Isaacs

PLATE 18. TRUMPET PHENOMENA
The trumpet held to mouth by an invisible connection.

CHAPTER XIV

ECTOPLASMIC STRUCTURES

THE photographs referred to in this chapter are ectoplasmic structures physically constructed for various purposes. The following chapter dealing with voice boxes is closely connected with these structures and both chapters should be considered together.

It is desirable that definitions should be clearly understood. The term "psychic rod" has been generally applied to all such forms of ectoplasmic emanations.

The photographs obtained, and very close observance of the various forms of phenomena in which a force external from the medium is employed, now definitely permit of two main classifications, i.e., "ectoplasmic arms" and "ectoplasmic rods".

The structures photographed are ectoplasmic arms.

Nevertheless, it is not possible to draw a distinct line between an arm and a rod, as an arm can be instantly converted into a rod when required.

The function of the arms is to act as a "power cable" for the construction of voice boxes, either in the trumpet or attached to the medium. In the latter instance the arm is used to convey the sounds from the voice box to the trumpet for amplification. These formations are also used in the process of apporting objects, conveying them in a dematerialized condition through the "arm" to the trumpet, where rematerialization is effected.

When at times these arms have come in contact with sitters they have been felt to be soft and flexible, slightly warm and coarse in texture. They are able to grip objects (Plate No. 21 shows the gripper-like tentacles at the end of the arm). When an arm lifts a trumpet or other light object, the control of the object is weak. In Plate No. 19 the arm had been connected to a trumpet, the trumpet was too weak to hold it, and it fell to the floor by the side of the sitter. The author has at times helped the trumpet to rest on his lap for photographs by gently raising the knees so that the trumpet would not fall off (see Plate No.19). These photographs provide corroboration for the descriptions of similar "tubular" or "ribbon" (Plate No. 20) formations with "sucker-like" tentacles at the extremities, witnessed through the mediumship of Rudy Schnieder.

The possibility must not be overlooked that levitation of an object may be assisted by a rod which is withdrawn immediately prior to an exposure.

On several occasions the ends of the arms have been illuminated. By a very high vibration the extreme. Tips of the arms are shown as a blue ring of light. It is important to mention here that the light is in a ring formation with a dark centre. (See "Voice Production.")

When this phenomenon has been produced there have been two such lights, which move about in a controlled manner. Firstly, they are shown near the solar plexus, then they move out away from the medium to the sides, forward, and above his head. When the Guide has been asked to elevate them they have risen above the head, and when asked to move them forward, they have moved forward, and so on. At one sitting the illuminated end descended in a circular movement to the mouth of a trumpet standing just in front of the medium. The trumpet rose in the air and moved freely round the sitters; the blue light being seen the whole time at the trumpet's mouth. Finally, the trumpet was returned to the floor and the blue ring of light was seen to rise from the trumpet and return to the solar plexus in an arc-like movement.

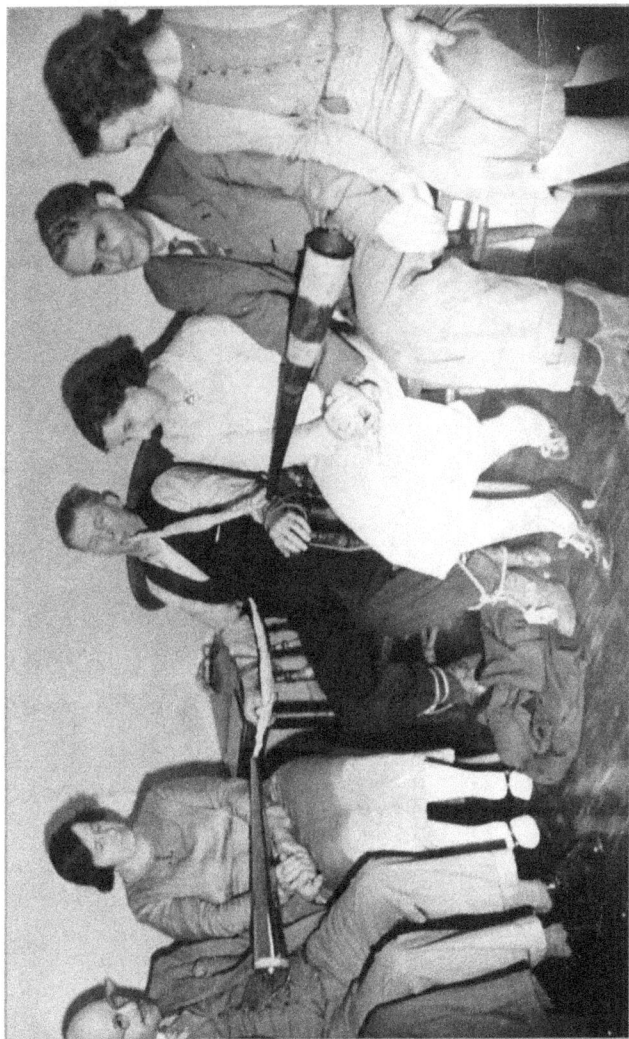

PLATE 19. ECTOPLASMIC ARMS

Leon Isaacs

The trumpets are connected by two ectoplasmic arms, one from the medium's mouth and the other from the solar plexus.

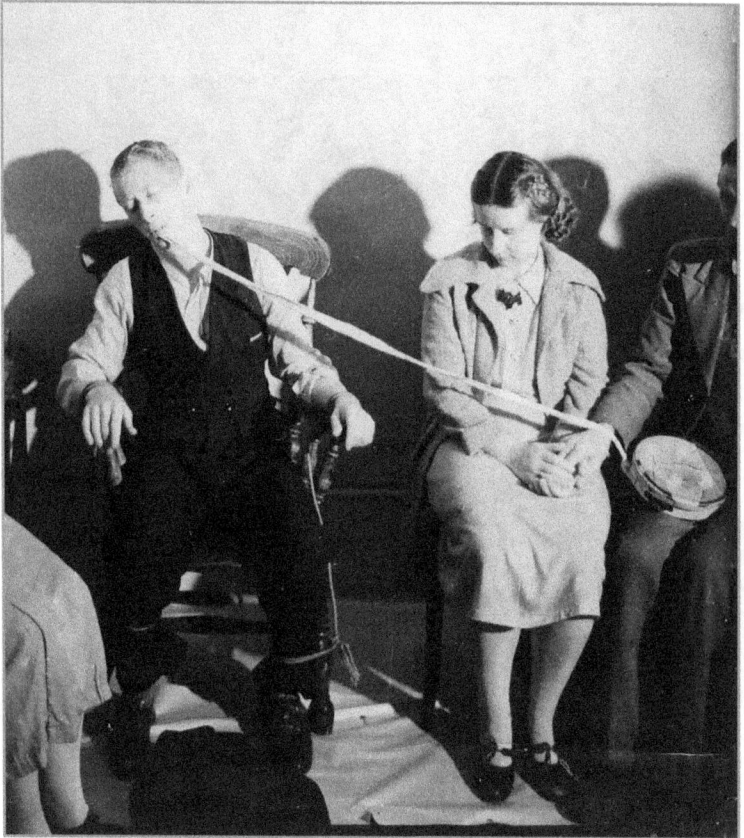

Daily Mirror Photographer

PLATE 20. ECTOPLASMIC ARMS

*An ectoplasmic arm of "ribbon" formation attached to a
tambourine,*

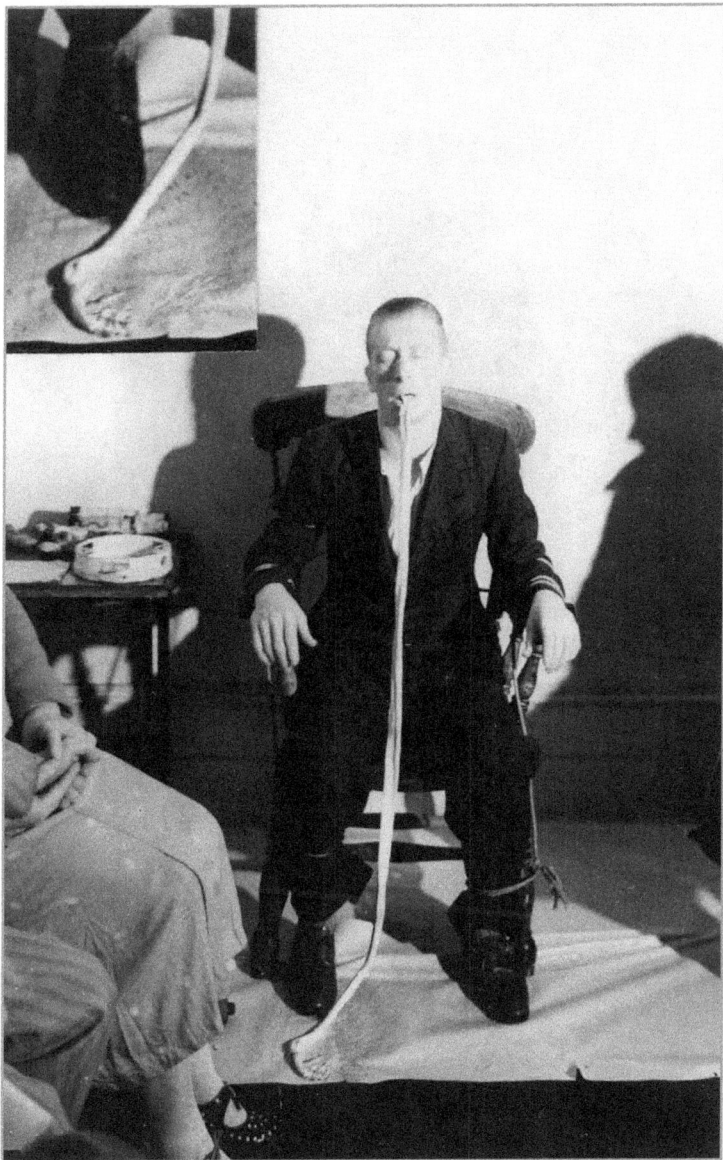

Daily Mirror Photographer

PLATE 21. ECTOPLASMIC ARMS

*"Grippers" at the end of an ectoplasmic arm for clasping
objects. Note the orifice above the "grippers".*

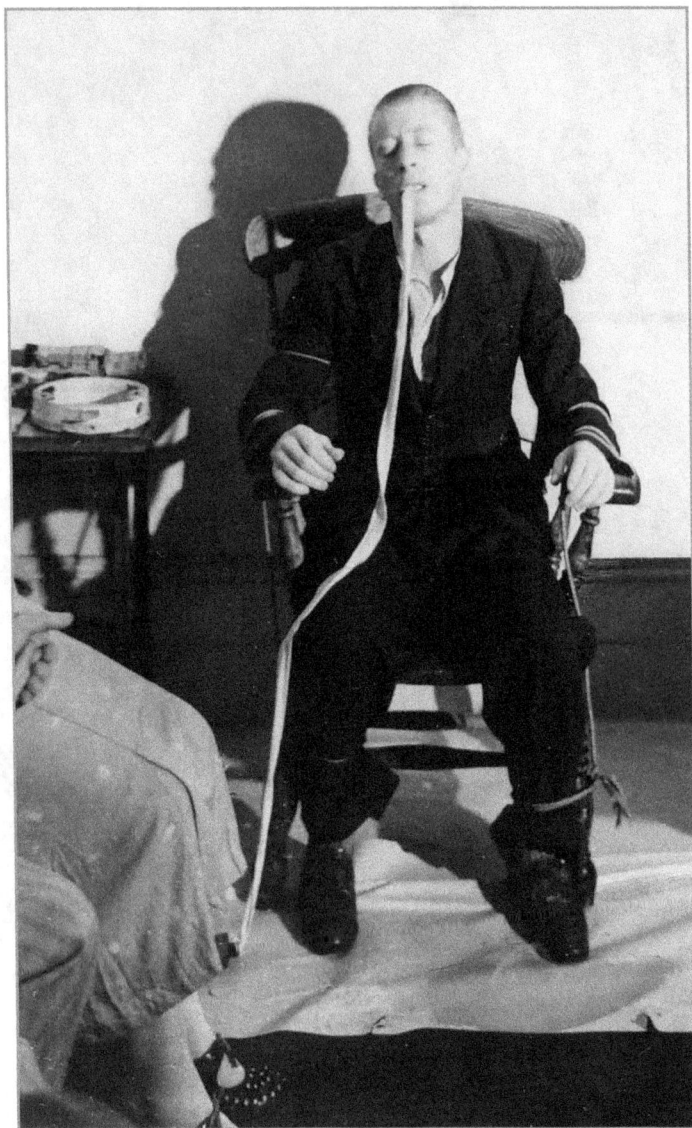

Daily Mirror Photographer

PLATE 22. ECTOPLASMIC ARMS

*An ectoplasmic arm of "ribbon" formation attached to the
mouth of a trumpet.*

Quite different is the function of the ectoplasmic "rod". This is used for strong movement and for the levitation of heavy articles. It has not yet been possible to photograph one of these "rods". The Guide (Black Cloud) has given the following reason for this. Rods are often invisible and cannot therefore be photographed. If the rods were to be brought into a physical condition they would appear as shafts of light; if the vibration was still further reduced to create a physical object, it would simply photograph as an ectoplasmic arm. The emission of the infra-red ray and the very dull red glow that accompanies it, "dissolves" the rod instantly.

It must, however, be placed on record that rods have been seen by sitters. In the many and varied conditions under which séances are held, there has at times been a slight degree of daylight seen through the general darkness where a window has not been covered with a thoroughly opaque material. The general darkness created was sufficient for the Guides to work in, but to eyes attuned to the darkness a less dense black area is observable under these conditions. When this situation has existed and objects are in levitation, passing over this area, a strong thick straight structure is seen attached to the object in levitation, the circumference of which may vary from three to six inches.

The less dark area is at times a fanlight, and the levitated object being so high in the air it would be absolutely impossible for the medium to have secreted a sufficiently sizable piece of mechanism about his person to accomplish such a levitation.

On other occasions, luminous objects may be on the floor, and the rods can be seen, as described, against the lighted surfaces.

At one sitting the author saw, against a very dimly illuminated area lit up by the glow of luminous paint, a rod extending from the ceiling straight down to the far side of the medium. This looked like a plank, about four inches wide (the thickness could not be gauged), but this structure was perfectly straight and precise, the edges being as clean-cut as a rule.

Again, in a very dim red light a structure has been seen by all sitters emerging from the solar plexus region as thick as the trunk of a medium-sized tree about eight to ten inches wide at the base close to the body and slowly tapering off to where the trumpet joined it.

Experience in sittings has given further knowledge of these rods. When a trumpet has been temporarily rested upon the lap of the sitter, three or four places removed from the medium, and is again taken into use, the rod has been felt across the linked hands or knees of the sitters. It is felt to be rigid and extremely strong, as may be gathered from the downward pressure that the sitters in question have experienced. It can best be likened to a rod of iron.

These rods are capable of very great strength. At times a trumpet has been pressed against a sitter, forcing him back into his chair in spite of every effort to resist. A solid mahogany table so heavy that it takes two people to lift it, has been taken from a corner of the room and deposited in the centre of the circle. At a Christmas Tree Party for spirit children held at the Balham Psychic Society, at which sixty people were present, the tree had been fastened into a wooden crate. The crate was nailed to the floor with eight-inch nails through pieces of timber four inches thick. The tree was also nailed with similar nails to other pieces of four-inch quartering which, in turn, were nailed to the sides of the crate. The tree was further wedged in with wood, etc. At the end of this séance, after almost every toy had been played with, musical instruments played in harmony with the singing, clockwork toys wound up and set working, and every toy on the tree had been taken off (there were over a hundred toys), the tree was wrenched out of the fastenings, pulling up the floor-boards in doing so, levitated to the skylight, where it partially pulled off the brown paper that had been fixed to make the church light-proof, and finally gently descended in the dark, crowded hall to rest between two sitters. This Christmas tree was ten feet high.

Rods used in a séance for levitation of objects are straight, and movement is the same as would result from movement of a ball-and-socket joint.

The gripping of objects by the rods is instantaneous; one object may be in levitation and deposited, and as the act of deposition takes place, a second object nearby may be immediately raised with great vigour.

The levitation of the medium to considerable heights and distances in halls, etc., also indicates the strength of the psychic power used.

Although the use of rods for levitation is the main method used, the movement of objects in a séance is not confined to this means, as may be seen by referring to the chapter on Materialized Forms, Heads, Hands, etc.

CHAPTER XV

VOICE PRODUCTION

THE production of a spirit-voice, unassociated with the medium's vocal organ, takes place in a "voice-box" produced in ectoplasm or by other means.

The photographs show the ectoplasmic formations housing the voice mechanism. The Guides inform us that a replica of the medium's vocal organs is built in the structure. For such a physical formation to be built up with Mr Webber, a complete trance state is essential, and the Guides' instruction must be accepted. When photographs have been secured of voice-boxes through other mediums, they show a similarity of structure.

Plates Nos. 24 and 25 bear a very close resemblance to photographs of voice-boxes obtained in New York some years ago through the mediumship of Mrs Margery Crandon. It is noteworthy that, when similar photographs are taken with a number of years intervening in places as far apart as London and New York, through different mediums, with different controls, *prima facie* evidence exists of a common fund of knowledge from which the Guides are able to obtain instruction.

It is definitely established that voices do emanate from these formations, as is proved by the hearing of weaker-toned words in the immediate proximity of the medium, while at the same time the words are being loudly produced by amplification in the trumpet a considerable distance away from the medium, the dim voice resembling the volume of sound one hears from a gramophone sound-box disconnected from the amplifier.

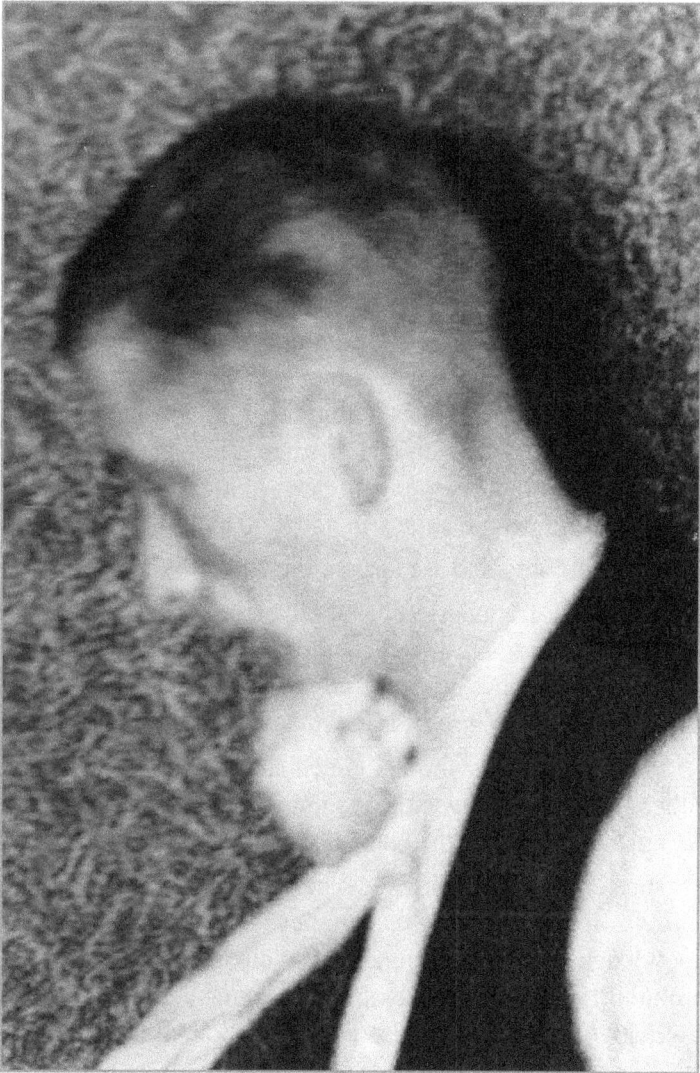

PLATE 23. ECTOPLASMIC VOICE-BOXES.

*A voice-box with an ectoplasmic arm. Note the merging of
ectoplasmic surround into the throat.*

Proof that the spirit-voice cannot be the product of the medium's vocal organ lies in the fact that, while the spirit-voice is speaking, the Guide can often be heard speaking through the medium's throat simultaneously.

Further evidence that voices must be produced through a mechanism external to the medium is demonstrated when two spirit conversations are taking place at the same time in different parts of the room, while the Guide is also using the; human throat. Thus, one often hears three voices, each distinct in its tonal quality from the others, simultaneously.

When such phenomena are produced the trumpets carrying the spirit-voices are on each side of the room and the source of the voice at these times lies within the mouth of the trumpet, so that the voice mechanism is constructed very near to or within the trumpet mouth—the trumpets being connected to the medium by an ectoplasmic arm and held by an ectoplasmic rod.

Voices so obtained are termed the "direct voice".

Voices are frequently produced, clearly and distinctly and without the use of a trumpet; these are called "independent voices". No specific evidence has yet been obtained to indicate what mechanism is used for the independent voice.

The photographs show, in each case, that the voice-box is either attached directly to the medium, or by an ectoplasmic arm. An arm also connects the voice-box to the mouth of the trumpet.

The sounds created in the voice-box have to travel along the ectoplasmic arm to the trumpet for amplification. Our knowledge of how the sound so travels is not conclusive. The probability is that the ectoplasmic arm is tubular. Another alternative is that the ectoplasmic connection possesses a quality that carries sound waves, which are again translated into audibility by a mechanism such as a diaphragm constructed in the trumpet.

Evidence in support of the thesis that the ectoplasmic arms are tubular is seen on Plate No. 21, where just above the grippers

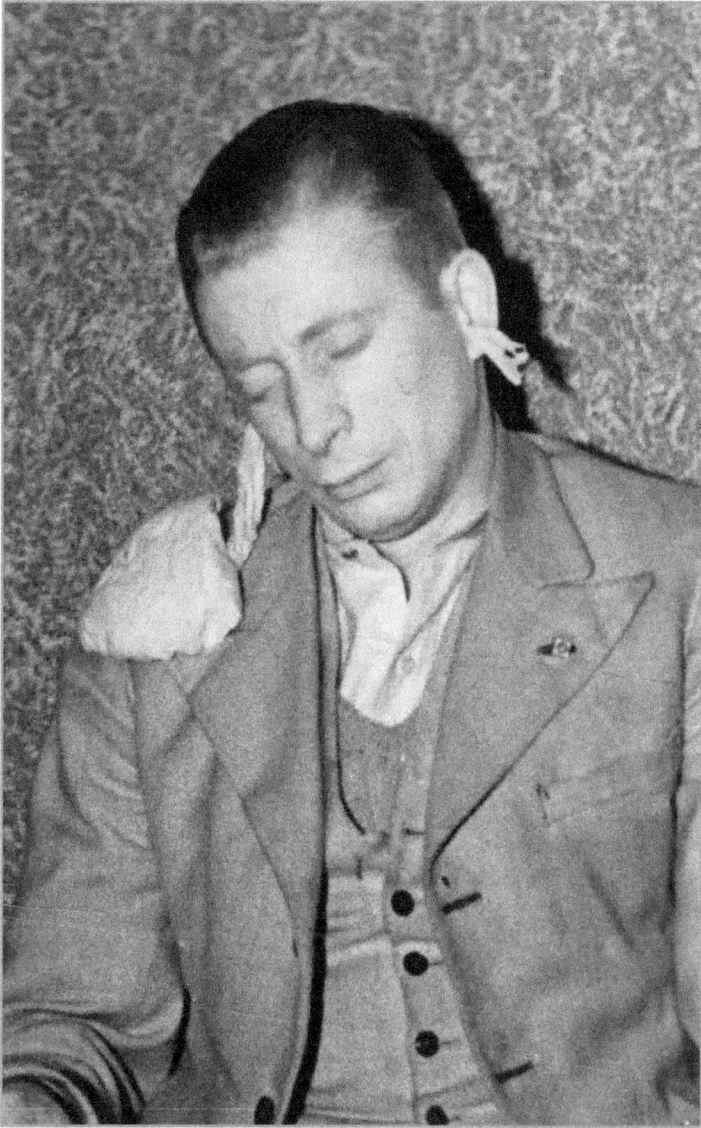

Leon Isaacs

PLATE 24. ECTOPLASMIC VOICE-BOXES.
Voice-box showing the source of emergence at the ear.
Ectoplasm is also seen emerging from the other ear.

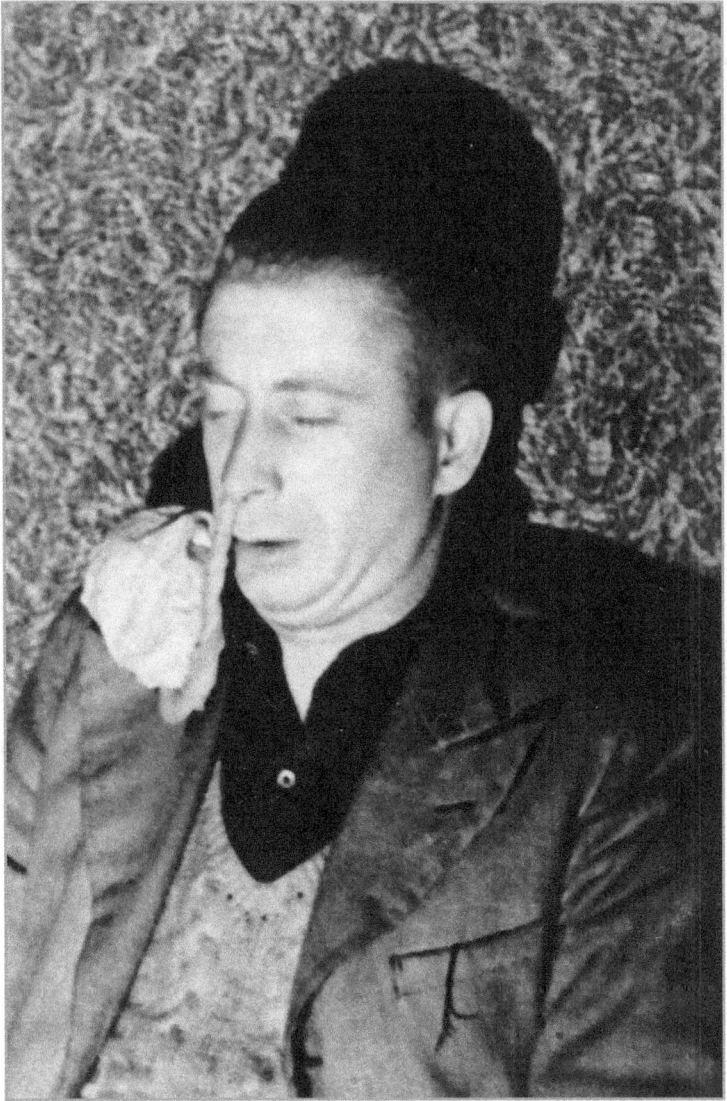

Harry Edwards

PLATE 25. ECTOPLASMIC VOICE-BOXES.

Voice-box with the source of emergence at nostril. Similar formation photographed in America with Margery Crandon.

a mouth-like orifice is seen, presenting an appearance of hollowness throughout the arm. The statement in the previous chapter that when the ends of these arms were illuminated, they appeared as rings of light, gives further support to the contention that the arms may be hollow. The Guides also speak of "hollow rods".

Definite statements can be made as to the way in which sounds are produced through the voice-boxes.

As the replica of human vocal organs are reproduced, so is a wind-instrument created, requiring a current of air to vibrate the mechanism.

When a vigorous, loud, and sustained voice is heard coming through a trumpet, the sound of air emission can also be distinguished, consonant with the deep breathing of an orator. This is particularly noticeable with a strong singing voice.

The method by which the air current is directed through the voice-box has not yet been ascertained. It may be (a) passed through the medium's body; (b) travel from the body via the ectoplasmic arm; or (c) emanate from the atmosphere adjacent to the medium.

As regards the latter, it should be remembered that a phenomenon common to most forms of physical mediumship is that strong currents of air are experienced, sometimes of great force. These currents of air come from the proximity of the medium, and curtains are blown horizontal to their fastenings. They are much colder than the general atmosphere. Therefore, the possibility exists that the current of air required to create sound may be obtained from a source external to the medium.

More tenable is the thesis that the air current is supplied through the medium's body to the voice-box. This is confirmed by the statement above that respiratory sounds are heard with vigorous singing. Furthermore, as aported objects and ectoplasm can be emitted through the physical body so could a volume of air be transmitted. This need not interfere with the operating of the human throat by the Guide in control, which is often heard speaking while spirit-voices are also present.

A feature of Mr Webber's mediumship is the singing of hymns and ballads through the trumpet or in the independent voice. One control, Reuben, possesses an extremely powerful voice, so strong that at times the trumpet is in a condition of tension, setting up such a high vibration that it takes on a ringing tone. At all times the direct voice is of full loud-speaker strength, possessing a quality of tone that is distinctive, and which the medium is incapable of reproducing. Each syllable is clearly articulated. If the medium could produce this singing voice normally, he could obtain a good living on the concert platform without endangering his life and health at public séances.

Reuben has sung continuously for an hour without cessation, with such vigour that any human throat would have become exhausted and hoarse. His rendering of hymns has been recorded by the Decca Record Co., Ltd.[1]

Clearly too, but without such force, Paddy (a boy control) is often heard, as is also the rich contralto voice of a lady, and other spirit singers. A phenomenon (impossible for human agency to reproduce) is the singing of Reuben and Paddy at the same time through the same trumpet—one voice a powerful rich baritone, and the other a thin piping voice. When these controls sing, the voice-box is definitely built in the small end of the trumpet. The trumpet is generally well away from the medium, six to eight feet high, and a similar distance in front of the medium. The origin of these voices lies within the trumpet. It is interesting to remember that the diameter of a trumpet's mouth is half an inch, and after use this end becomes battered and bent so that the orifice is partially closed. Under such conditions no human mouth could possibly use such a mouth-piece and produce the perfectly formed words of a hymn, slow, deliberate and perfectly enunciated.

---

1. The gramophone record of Reuben singing "Lead Kindly Light " and "There's a Land," 10-inch double-sided record, can be obtained from the Balham Psychic Research Society, 11 Childebert Road, London, S.W. 17, price 5s. 6d. [*Original footnote from 1940 and not available in 2018.*]

Reuben has also revealed a comprehensive knowledge of acoustics and the technical knowledge necessary for recording his voice through the microphone—he was responsible for giving instructions as to where the microphone should be placed and positioned the trumpet to avoid distortion. On one occasion, when Mr Hugh Millar was recording the voice, the trumpet in use was a two-piece one, producing a vibrant effect. Reuben discarded the trumpet and sang as clearly and as strongly in independent voice. No human throat could produce the resonant vibrant tone that is heard when Reuben sings.

It is not intended to give here details of the evidential nature of messages received—let it suffice that voices are heard with every kind of intonation and dialect; speech in foreign tongues has been given to visitors from other lands and conversations maintained in that tongue. Voices of men, women, and children are distinct, and the conversations display an intimate knowledge of family events that are personal to the sitter and the spirit communicant.

Our knowledge of the manner in which an independent voice is produced is limited. All that can be said here is that such voices are heard speaking clearly without trumpets, without physically constructed voice-boxes, in either darkness or white light. Independent voices have been obtained through other mediums without the need for those mediums to go into a deep or even partial trance.

On occasions when the medium has had a mishap, and is unconscious, with bleeding, and doubt has been felt as to the treatment or procedure to be adopted, and the light has been on, the voice of Black Cloud or Paddy has been heard giving instructions, the voices originating some feet away from the medium.

On one evening, when Mr Webber was away from home, Paddy's voice was heard speaking softly yet distinctly in three different rooms of the house. He was heard by people in each room, uttering the same words at the same time.

ADDENDUM, MARCH 1940

On February 10th, at Lincoln, a conversation was carried on via the trumpet in French. On January 27th, at the Sanctuary of St. Andrew, Harringay, conversations were carried on in Swedish, Portuguese, and a recital of Latin was given. The sitter who carried on the Swedish conversation said there was no trace of an accent foreign to the tongue. It may be re-emphasized here that Mr Webber was an unlettered man, he rarely read a book, in fact, his only reading matter was the newspapers and children's comics.

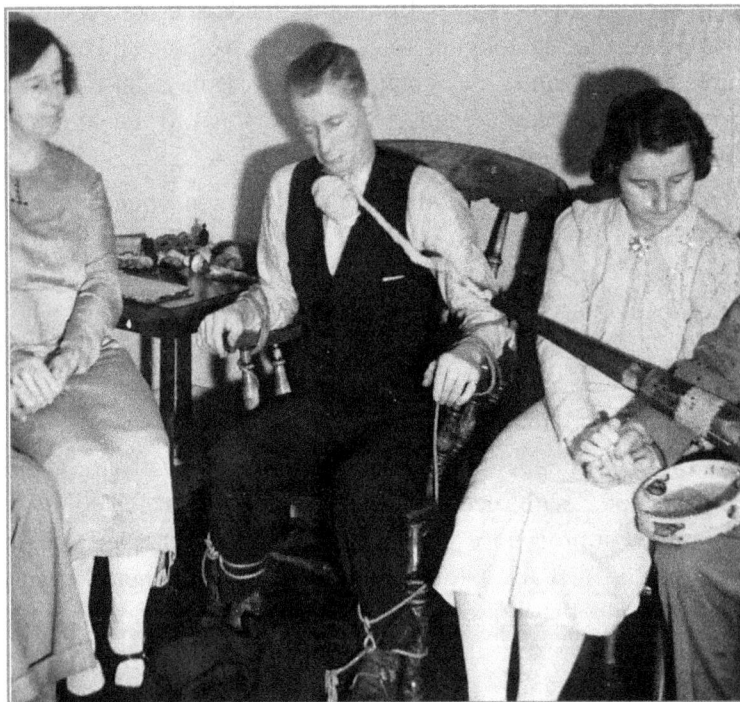

Leon Isaacs

PLATE 26. ECTOPLASMIC VOICE-BOXES.

A Voice-box near the throat with an ectoplasmic arm attached to the trumpet.

CHAPTER XVI

ECTOPLASMIC MATERIALS

THE ectoplasmic formations referred to in the photographs have been repeatedly produced in a reasonable red light, all sitters observing the phenomena. In dark séances, the process of emitting ectoplasm is often illustrated by means of the illuminated plaques.

The process is as follows: the medium's body is bent forward whilst in the ropes, so that his head is over his feet. From the mouth there commences to emerge a substance that to the eye looks like heavy vapour. As it emerges, it "unrolls" and pours down in front of the medium's body to the floor. At the same time, it continues to pour out from the mouth, like a cascade, until there is a considerable volume on the floor, spreading for several feet each way. The emergence is rapid, and the process of emission only occupies a few seconds. There is no noise from the medium's throat during this time.

Rapidly, in two to three seconds only, the vapourish mass condenses or becomes concentrated, until there hangs from the mouth a length of material-like substance.

The texture of this material varies according to the conditions prevailing at the sitting, and the condition of the medium himself. When conditions are good, the texture is very fine and close. When the conditions are not so good the material is coarser, and rents may be seen in the fabric. (See Plate No. 27, where a rent is visible.)

This material has often been handled, under the Guide's instructions, by the author and other sitters. It is moist, though

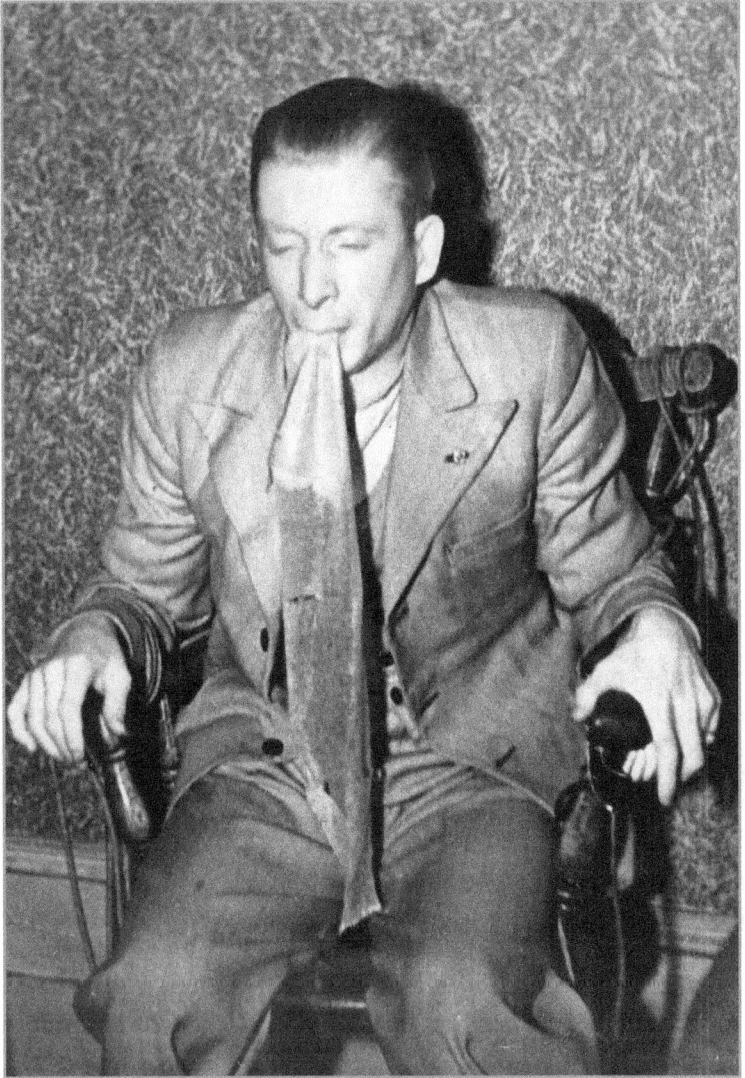

Leon Isaacs

PLATE 27. ECTOPLASMIC STRUCTURES

Ectoplasmic material—note the small rent.

not very wet, and possesses a peculiar odour. On a number of occasions, the author has been invited to unravel the material and open it out. To do this, however, extreme care has to be taken. The width of the material, when opened out, is wider than the outstretched arms of one person. Whilst unravelling the ectoplasm at a sitting, the author was unable to stretch it out to its full extent, and the assistance of the next sitter was allowed by the Guide. The full extent must have been two yards or more.

Plate No. 29 illustrates an occasion when sitters were permitted to take hold of the ectoplasmic material, and they were asked to open it out and hold it up so that a better idea of its area could be photographed. On occasions such as these sitters are a little nervous of causing harm, and here apparently, they did not use their two hands; the photograph, however, serves to show the considerable length of material produced.

The return of the ectoplasm is instantaneous. The author has had gentle hold of the material one moment, and within the second that followed, the material has been whisked away with a sound like the twang of a piece of elastic and it has disappeared.

On the occasion when the photograph, shown by Plate No. 30, was taken, a red light was burning, and the sitters saw this voluminous material passing back into the medium in a fraction of a second—one moment it was visible, and the next it had disappeared. Following the re-absorption of the material by the medium, a gulping throat action is heard.

Several descriptions of this material have been given by sitters, as "closely woven silk of a rich quality"; "like wet toy balloon rubber"; "a wide piece of thin seaweed".

This formation has no pattern, such as "net". It is like a skin rather than a woven fabric. It is distinct from the ectoplasmic drapery that enfolds a materialized form.

This drapery is most gossamer-like and is so light that its texture is as a spider's fine web. Each strand is composed of thirteen to fifteen minor strands, which are interwoven four

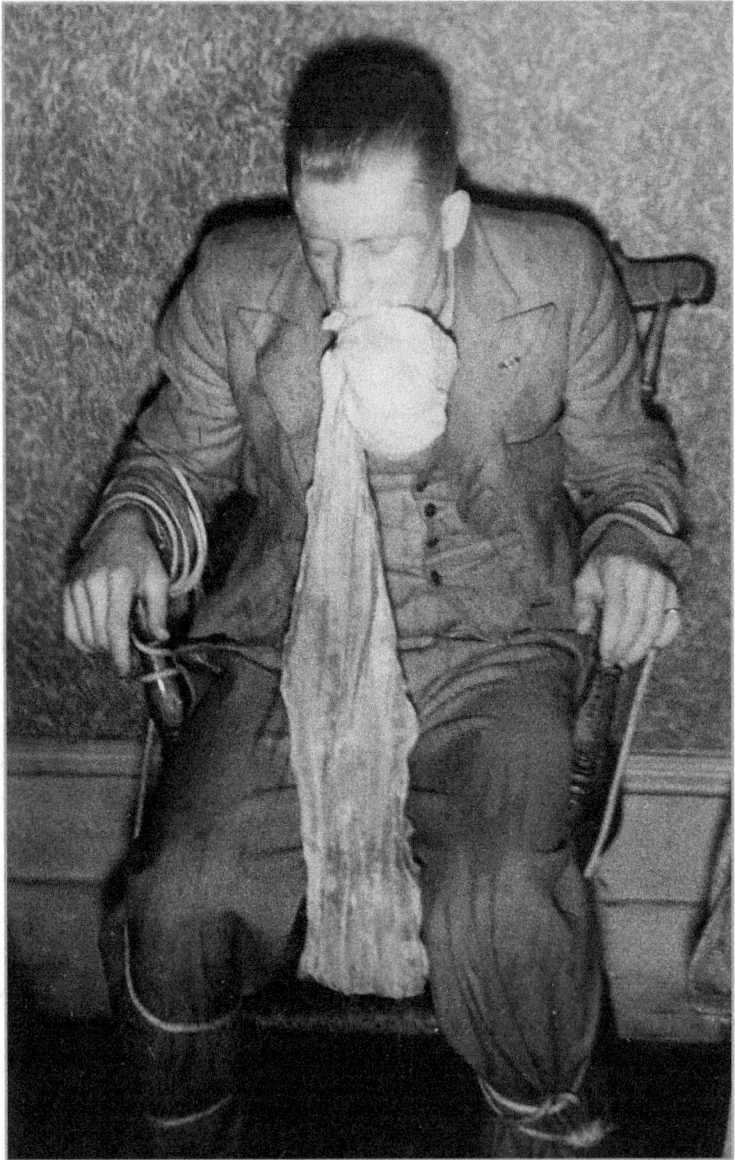

Leon Isaacs

PLATE 28. ECTOPLASMIC STRUCTURES
Ectoplasmic material with bunching at the mouth.

Harry Edwards

PLATE 29. ECTOPLASMIC STRUCTURES

A length of ectoplasmic material held up by sitters to show its length.

times around each side of the square forming the net pattern, and the size of the square is about the size of a pin's head: impossible to humanly produce.

The author has been told that the formations, as photographed, are composed of cells, and that they possess nerves and capillaries and are therefore sensitive. Whatever form ectoplasm may take, it is obviously of human content—it

Leon Isaacs

PLATE 30. ECTOPLASMIC STRUCTURES

*A length of ectoplasmic material taken upwards and backwards
to the wall.*

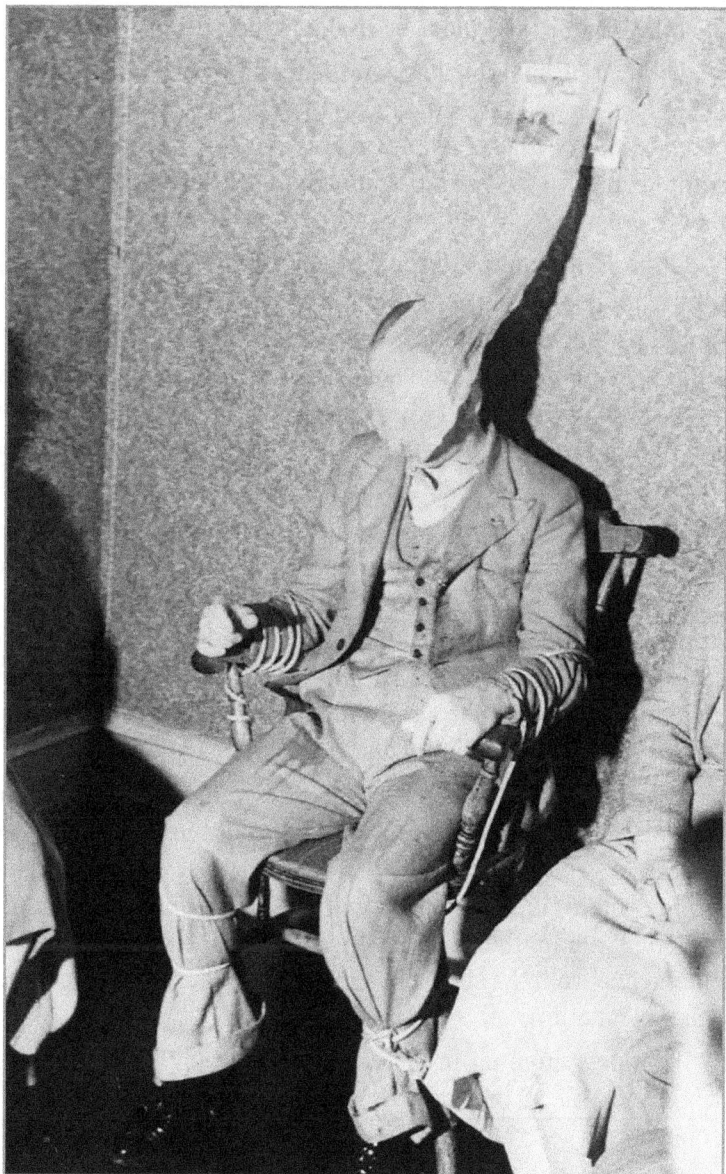

Leon Isaacs

PLATE 30a. ECTOPLASMIC STRUCTURES

Another view of Plate 30.

proceeds from the living body and returns to be absorbed into the body. It must therefore be living matter.

This ectoplasm is the basis for materialization of spirit people (see chapter on Materializations), though from observations taken whilst with Mr Webber, it is not clear what form the ectoplasm is in, to enable spirit people to use it to manifest themselves.

One of the controls (Dr Miller) has given the following information: first the ectoplasm is produced, then the controls mould it around the etheric body of the spirit visitor, who is able to draw from the ectoplasm that power to materialize the etheric body. In doing so, the body becomes as physical as in earthly life, with the various organs also materialized. Thus, the materialized etheric form is able to speak, etc.

At one sitting, ectoplasmic hands were seen to travel to the red lamp, take hold of it, and detach it from the ceiling hook. The bulb had a controlling switch in the fitting enabling it to be turned on and off at will by the spirit-controls. On this occasion the bulb was held, illuminating the ectoplasmic material, showing its texture, semi-transparent, and the complete absence of weaving marks—no threads or cross-threads were visible.

When this material is illuminated by means of luminous plaques, its texture is shadowy and does not show clear, defined edges. An ectoplasmic rod was shown this way, appearing straight and rigid, with bulges in it like "knuckles". The plaques travelled along the whole length of the rod, showing its emergence from the solar plexus, to the far end where an object was in levitation.

Trumpets, high up in the air, are also lit up by the plaques, which travel all round the trumpet to show no visible connection.

Plate No. 31 was obtained within two minutes of the commencement of a developing circle. Mr Webber had been bound to the chair and the white light put out, leaving the ruby lamp alight. The sitters had commenced to sing when Mr

Webber remarked: "There is something over my face; try a photograph." An exposure was made, resulting in the picture shown [below].

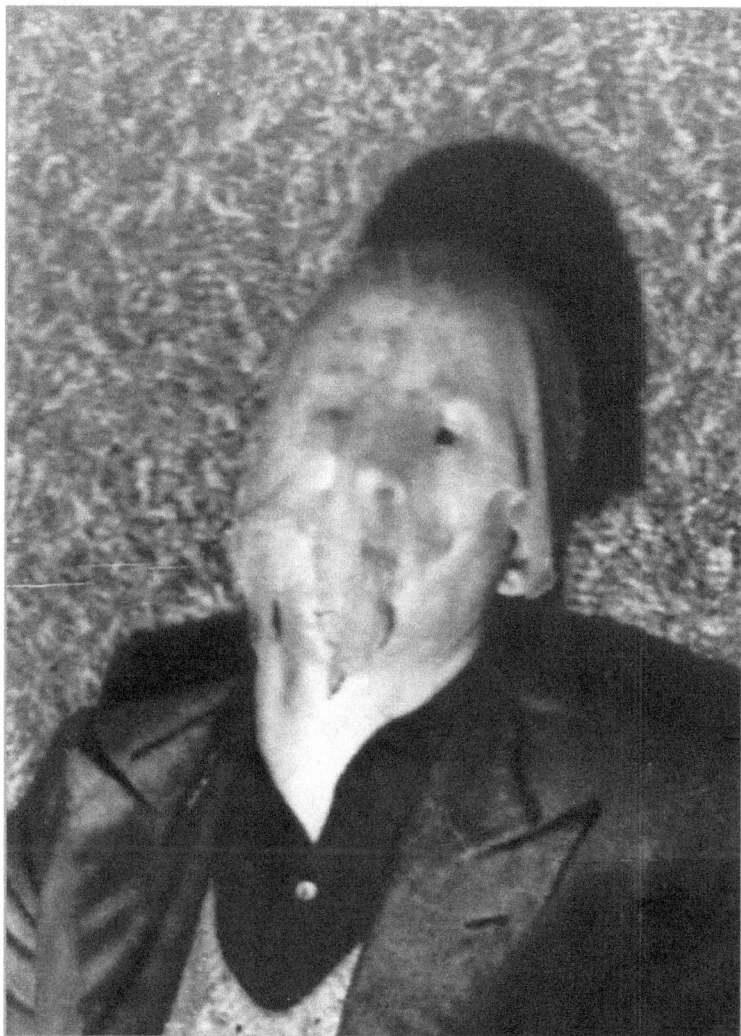

Harry Edwards

PLATE 31. ECTOPLASMIC STRUCTURES

This formation, with the source of emergence below the neck, was photographed while the medium was not in trance.

While levitation of objects in a white light is not uncommon, here is obtained (for the first time, it is believed) a photograph of ectoplasm in a physical state, taken with the medium "normal" in red light. The word normal is quoted, for while the medium was quite conscious of what was taking place, he was in an extremely sensitive condition.

After the exposure had been made, Black Cloud spoke in the "independent" voice, saying that when the plate was developed, "it would show ectoplasm over the head and face."

The source of the ectoplasmic emergence is from the body below the neck.

Later on, during this sitting, sitters in the circle felt their heads similarly enmeshed in ectoplasmic material, which stretched out from the medium. The circle, being a small one of seven sitters, saw, at one time, the floor space filled with ectoplasm, rising up round their legs. The atmosphere was very cold.

Plate No. 32 shows a length of ectoplasmic material over five yards long—the wide-angle lens of the camera could not receive the full length.

ADDENDUM, MARCH, 1940.

These two photographs of ectoplasmic formations were secured in January, 1940. They are remarkable for an unusual instruction from the Guide, eloquent of the improved technique the Guides were acquiring with the further development of the medium, illustrating the manner in which they were co-operating with the efforts to secure evidential photographs.

The author was in charge of the photographic apparatus and white light and all was ready to take a photograph should the opportunity come. The sitting was proceeding, and throat noises were heard coming from the medium, when the unusual instruction was received "photo and light."

A photograph being anticipated by the character of the throat-action noise, the infra-red was immediately flashed by pressing

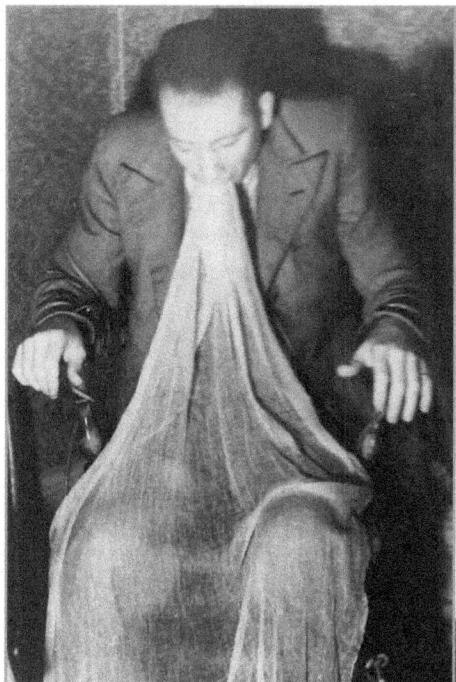

PLATE 32a.
*(Close up of part of
photograph below)*
*Photograph by
Harry Edwards*

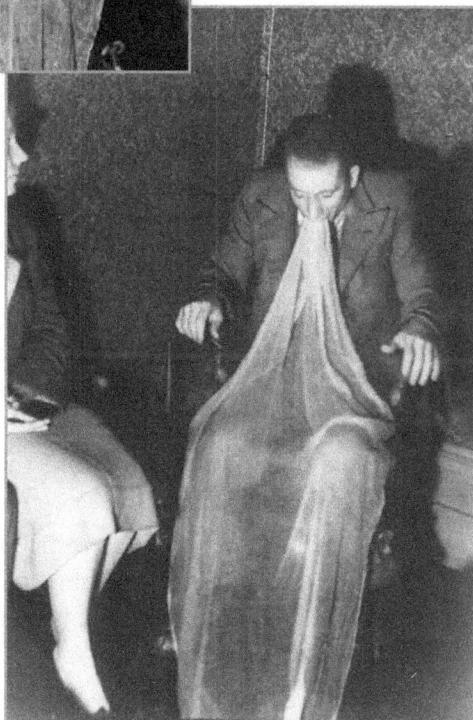

PLATE 32.
*(See opposite page
for explanation)*
*Photograph by
Harry Edwards*

the switch, the right hand came across and closed the shutter in front of the plate, returning to the white-lights switch. Both these switches are of the press kind, so that no delay was caused. Before the commencement of the sitting both these switches and the camera had been placed so conveniently that all could be worked quickly and without the necessity to rise from the chair. The three movements were therefore rapid, and the only interval between the photographic exposure and the white light was the time allowed to close the plate shutter. Two seconds is a generous time allowance.

Plate No. 33 was the first to be taken, and it will be realized that the absorption back into the medium of the ectoplasmic formation was therefore instantaneous.

It is obvious that it would be impossible for the medium in the photographed roped condition to dispose normally of the material requiring the use of his hands and to return to the roped position inside two seconds.

It would also have been impossible for any sitter to have taken and secreted the volume of material without unlinking hands, and other sitters becoming aware of the movement. Also, it is doubtful whether any sitter could have disposed of the material before the white light was switched on.

A few minutes later, after the plate had been changed and a new sashalite bulb inserted in the infra-red cabinet, a similar instruction was received "photo and light." On this occasion Plate No.34 was secured. The author was ready for this instruction, and the period between the infra-red flash and the white light was not more than one second, indeed the operation was so rapid that for a few moments the medium came back to normality.

It will be seen in this second photograph the expanse of ectoplasmic material is considerably greater, and the absorption back into the medium must have been an instantaneous action immediately after the exposure.

Harry Edwards

PLATE 33. ECTOPLASMIC STRUCTURES

The medium's head draped with ectoplasmic material. The white light was put on within 2 seconds of the photographic exposure.

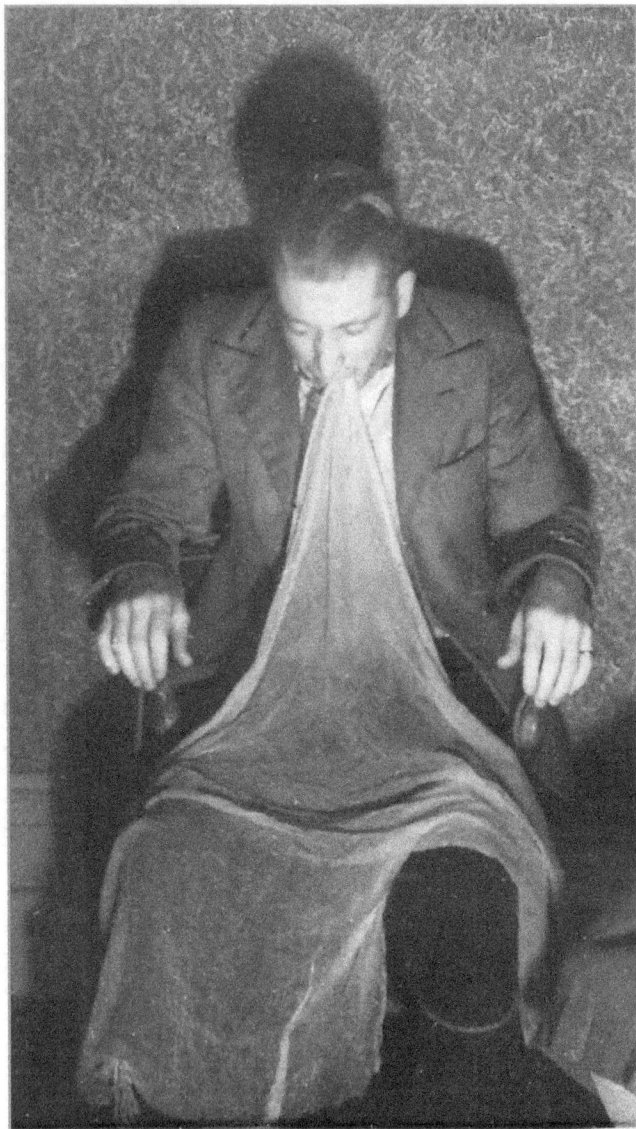

Harry Edwards

PLATE 34. ECTOPLASMIC STRUCTURES

*An expanse of ectoplasmic material photographed a few
minutes after Plate 33. White light was switched on one
second after the photographic exposure.*

It is hard to imagine a more perfect test condition for a medium than this, or more definite evidence of super-normal activity.

How completely these photographs dispose of the theory recently put forward that ectoplasm is a cheesecloth-like material, swallowed by the medium before the séance, regurgitated, and then re-swallowed! In the light of these photographs, and the time-factor, the absurdity of such a thesis is so obvious that no other comment is necessary.

Plans had been made to re-demonstrate this phenomenon before various scientific faculties and photographic societies, and this was only prevented by the passing of the medium.

It is confidently asserted, that these two photographs prove beyond doubt the existence of operating spirit intelligences possessing a knowledge of forces, anatomy, and laws entirely unknown to man.

124

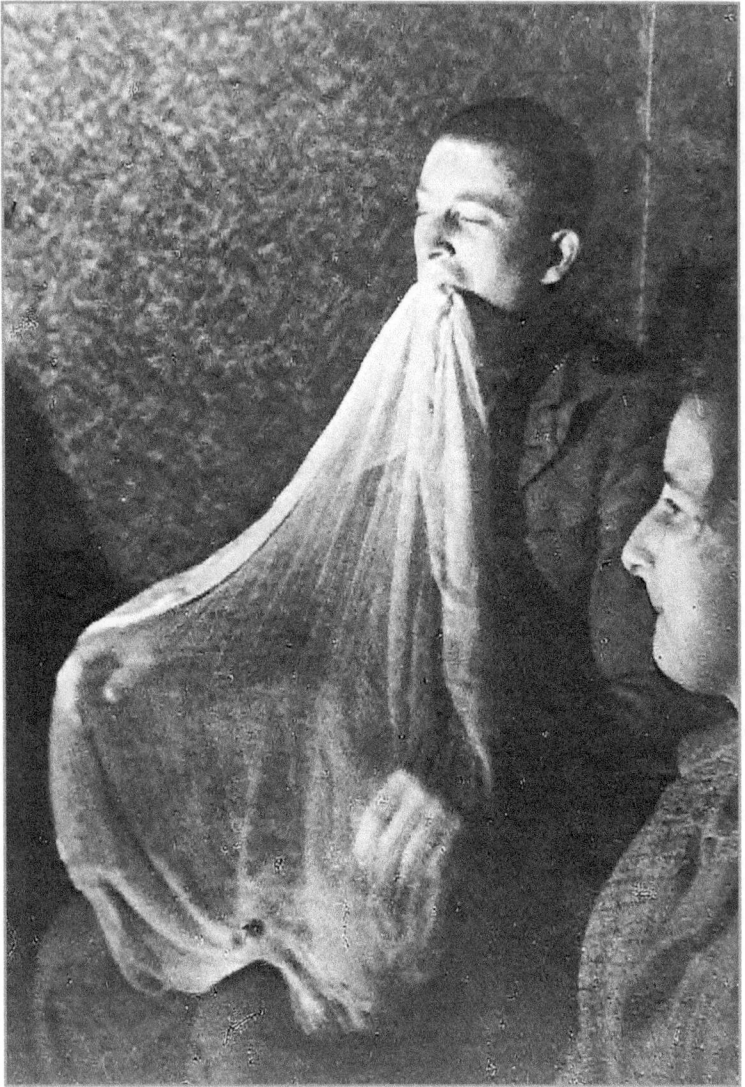

J. McCulloch

PLATE 35. ECTOPLASMIC STRUCTURES
A side view of ectoplasmic material.

CHAPTER XVII

MATERIALISED FORMS, HEADS, HANDS, ETC.

THE first phase of Mr Webber's mediumship to produce materialized forms was the creation of heads only, which were illuminated by means of the luminous plaques. With this development came hands, that were felt and seen by the sitters.

Looking into the heads full faced, they are seen to be of perfect formation; hair, eyes, nose, and mouth being fully physical.

The faces are often full-sized, but now and again are much smaller than any normal head, being about four to five inches high.

A white ectoplasmic cowl invariably surrounds the head, and the shape of shoulders and garments can be glimpsed in the illumination.

The period of formation occupies only a few seconds. When the plaque first illuminates the head, it may not be perfectly formed, but it rapidly assumes the correct features.

The heads remain in the proximity of the medium, probably linked to the medium by an ectoplasmic connection. They can, however, travel about six feet from the medium in any direction.

After the head has formed and a short period of time has elapsed, the lips are seen to move, and sounds like a preliminary struggle for articulation ensues. This finally leads to the materialization speaking to the sitters. This speech is usually perfectly audible, and the difference between that of a woman, a child, a man, or a Guide is quite distinctive.

The forms of Guides build up strongly, particularly so with the controls of the medium, in which case the voice is loud and clear.

These heads have been recognized very many times by sitters as the faces of those whom they knew when on earth.

Guides are often able to give further details of their personality, either showing head-dresses, colouring of features, or speaking in their own tongues. Conversations have taken place in tongues other than English between a materialized head and a sitter. If a person passed over as the result of head injuries, bandages, and blood-stains are reproduced to add weight to the identity.

Hands of all sizes are also seen by the plaques, and if in an instance of this nature there had been a deformity in physical life, such as the loss of a number of fingers or enlarged joints, these are faithfully reproduced.

Sometimes as many as five or six forms may be seen at a séance; at others, there may be materialized only one head, or not any at all.

The copious white ectoplasmic cowling is evidential of supernormal power apart from the heads themselves. So voluminous is it that it would be difficult for any person to secrete it. Mr Webber is always open to a search; in fact, after there has been shown excessive cowling or drapery, the Guide invariably asks the chairman of the séance to search the medium before he leaves the presence of the sitters.

Frequently, hands are felt by sitters. They are full physical hands. The large hand of a powerful man or the small hand of a child. They are, as a rule, slightly wet, yet their temperature is warmer than the hands of the sitters themselves. The latter through being linked for an hour or more are usually hot, yet the materialized hand is the warmer. If the hands are of Chinese Guides, the long nails which these Guides have can be felt by the sitters.

Sometimes the hands caress the face, hands, and arms of a sitter, or they may play with the hair or an ornament.

There is another phase of materialization that is worthy of comment. In a dark séance a cigarette lighter has been flicked on, and in the white flash there has been outlined the solid form of a being with outstretched arm—one of the medium's controls.

At times, when the sitters are known to the Guide, or it is judged they will not be alarmed by a little frivolity, jokes are played. On one occasion Mr Bernard Gray, of the Sunday Pictorial, who was present at the séance, had his hair lightly tied to that of the author. If there should be spare rope or string, a sitter may find himself or herself securely tied. (See "The Securing of the Medium.")

Thus, the fact has to be taken into account that at times there may be present in the circle the materialized forms of the medium's controls who are carrying out work in connection with the phenomena. The author has not yet excluded from his mind the work of controls in this state of being responsible for the joining of two parts of a trumpet together, removing the spectacles from a sitter's face, and perhaps assisting with the final stage of removing the coat from the medium.

At the present time, the developing circle is sitting in red light for materializations, and the physical forms have been seen, felt, and conversed with. During such phenomena the medium is often seen bound to his chair.

With materialization, at first a vague, shadowy form is seen, darker than the prevailing light. This form then becomes denser, and the hands and head are held to the red light for closer examination. The red light is about nine feet from the floor, yet the materialized people are able to rise to it and expose their heads in close proximity to the bulb.

Reuben and Paddy materialize most easily. At one circle Reuben materialized perfectly. He took hold of the author's hand and passed it over his face. This was repeated with other sitters. It was noticed that Reuben's hands were very warm. A conversation also took place between Reuben and those present. Thus not only is a physical figure present, but the lungs and larynx must also have been formed.

The warmth experienced in materialization raises an interesting problem. From whence does the warmth come? Ectoplasm as felt, is wet and cold, yet it is from this substance that the forms build themselves. One reasonable hypothesis is that the ectoplasm is in a state of very high vibration, and just as the infra-red ray is the transition stage between light and heat (there is always heat with the infra-red ray) so it may be that the condition of "vibration" (for want of a more expressive word), which is used for the purpose of materializations may give the heat that is certainly in evidence.

When a form has built up in the red light, its disappearance is of interest. Standing full length in the centre of the circle, it is seen to diminish downwards as if passing through the floor. The period of time necessary for the disappearance is about two seconds. After the disappearance of a form, throat action is heard from the medium—gulp-like sounds, rather similar to those made when ectoplasm is returning to the medium's body.

On the occasion previously referred to, when the red light was detached from the fitting, it was used to light up the faces of materialized people, the lamp being held close to, and almost touching, the faces, so that there could be no possible doubt at all as to the form being present.

Three forms have been seen at the same time, in a moderate degree of red light—two of the forms were full length, while the third, quite small, was of Paddy, a boy of about ten years old.

At most séances a small spirit child, answering to the name of Matilda, skips with a rope, and obeys requests for fast skipping, hopping, etc.

The following are extracts from published reports, by independent persons, dealing with this phenomenon:

"Jack Webber gave four remarkable séances at Cambridge. . . He came alone and only arrived a short time before the first séance . . . so there was no chance of anything being arranged beforehand. Several well-known people were present, including an Indian Prince (Prince Deo), and the Dean of Trinity College. Some members of the Cambridge Society for Psychical Investigation were present at each séance.

The sittings were carried out under test conditions. No restrictions were made as to the method of tying, in fact, he was tied so tightly one evening that some of the sitters complained that it might stop his circulation. But Jack just said: 'That's all right, let it go.'

On three nights, materialized heads appeared, and although some of these heads were perfectly formed they were considerably smaller than normal size. The most remarkable materialization occurred when the head of an Indian came close to me, the features showing clearly above the luminous slate.

The head bowed, and when I asked him if he could tell me his name, he said 'Ranji,' which, of course, was the name by which Prince Ranjitsinhji was known when he was up at Cambridge at the height of his fame as a cricketer. I knew him quite well when he was up at the University.

(Mr A.J. Case, President of the Cambridge Research Society, reporting in the Psychic News, *August 12th, 1939.)*

"For me, the most outstanding event of the séance was the materialization of two faces. A luminous plaque rose from the floor, and came within a few inches of my face: rising from it, partially concealed in what appeared to be a shining band of material, some two inches wide, was the face of a woman —I should estimate her to be between forty and fifty years of age: the face was perhaps a little larger than three-quarters life-size, and near enough for me to observe the fine moulding of the features, which were illuminated with the glow from the plaque. Particularly, I noticed the nose and nostrils, which seemed to be perfectly chiselled as from alabaster or some similar material.

The face was quite solid —three-dimensional, without colouring, but obviously alive; I encouraged it to talk while it floated there, resting on the plaque which was quite unsupported. The lips moved in an attempt to answer me, but produced strange 'ticking' sounds that seemed to precede any attempt at speech on these occasions. Eventually the woman whispered: 'I have no pain now, I do not suffer as I used to . . . isn't it glorious . . . Mother.' . . . Then the plaque withdrew and the face disappeared.

The woman's face was remarkable for the fine moulding of the features—almost like a piece of Greek sculpture; the absence of skin creases probably accentuated this, and while it was obviously the face of a mature woman, there was a suggestion of youthfulness about it. The eyes were partly in shadow, owing to the lighting arising from the plaque, so that it was difficult to determine whether or not they had been materialized: yet during the whole time the face remained there—a matter of several minutes—there was no suggestion of eyeless sockets.

The second face, which appeared after an interval . . . also came across to within a few inches of my face, supported by the luminous plaque.

This time the strong masculine features were surmounted with a white, typically Egyptian headdress: the long Roman nose gave the face a look of severity, and the eyes—what I could see of them, looked piercingly into mine. This face was unlike its predecessor in that there was a suggestion of swarthiness about it. Pronounced facial ridges in the flesh enhanced the severe expression, and the set of the jaw and mouth suggested a powerful character.

Several times the head bowed in front of me, and, projecting from the head-dress I noticed a triangular device which stood out and threw a shadow back on the forehead. I heard other sitters commenting on the 'hair'; they apparently overlooked this triangular projection, which had its base in the head-dress, and apex standing well out from the head. It seemed to be constructed from different material and was evidently not intended to be overlooked. I commented on it, and, after remaining in front of me for a brief period, the head withdrew and disappeared.

This, too, was solid, and three-dimensional in appearance, certainly more life-like than the first, nearer to life-size, and without the mask-like appearance that characterized the first, before it spoke.

Needless to say, there were no sitters in the room resembling either face. I later learned that the device in the head-dress corresponded to that worn by priests and officials of the ancient Egyptian temples: it apparently signified rank in the temple—this no doubt explains the repeated endeavours of the head to draw my attention to the device."

(*Special reporter for the* Two Worlds, *published January 27th, 1939·*)

"In the course of the séance there were five materialized heads shown against an illuminated plaque; they came to within an inch of our faces. They were not more than half the size of a normal head. Some of these were Guides who announced themselves by name, and such names were quite unknown to Mr Webber."

(*W. H. Glaser,* Two Worlds, *March 3rd, 1939.*)

"Three faces then materialized and came within a few inches of my eyes, and they were definitely smaller than Jack Webber's face."

(*Sid. C. Carter,* Two Worlds, *March 3rd, 1939.*)

ADDENDUM, MARCH 1940.

In February, 1940, the Guide asked for the floor to be covered with white powder. This was done. In the red light the medium and the white floor was clearly seen. Materialized forms were seen more easily against the white background. After the séance it was seen that the powder had not been disturbed, proving that the physical materialized forms did not touch the floor, but "floated". This peculiar gliding movement of materialized people has often been commented on with other materialization mediums, and the above experiment tends to confirm that they do not contact the floor.

This raises an interesting point, for as the materialized individuals are definitely physical for the time being, they do not obey the law of gravity.

Plate No. 36 was obtained in February, 1940, at a sitting specially arranged for the South London Press, when two editors and another representative were present. The photograph shows a perfect materialized hand emerging (probably) from the solar plexus region. On this occasion another photograph was secured (and published by the newspaper) showing the medium's hands held by the two editors, while the coat was removed from the body, similar to Plate No. 6. This newspaper published a laudatory article on the mediumship, as indeed has every other newspaper that has investigated it. It is pertinent to remember that newspaper men are, as a rule, of the hard, sceptical turn of mind, and invariably extremely critical of physical phenomena, and attend with the idea of "seeing through" the demonstration. On no occasion, however, has any newspaper investigator even queried the genuineness of the mediumship—all have testified to their bewildered amazement, and have reported the séances fairly.

Harry Edwards

PLATE 36. A MATERIALIZED HAND

*A materialized hand produced at a sitting specially arranged
for the Press.*

CHAPTER XVIII

INCIDENTS OF THE MEDIUMSHIP

THE following selected extracts are taken from the Psychic Press and other publications.

"At Birmingham, twenty-six roses were apported into the circle through closed doors and windows and were distributed to the twenty-six sitters. (The number of people sitting was not determined until the very last moment.)

"Psychic News, July 8th, 1939."

"At Birkbeck, there was a novel experiment. A bowl of water was placed on a locked piano and a jug of water on a gramophone cabinet. Despite the fact that both instruments were well beyond the medium's reach, Webber's Guides managed to place a record on the gramophone turntable and play it, and also to play the piano.

" *Psychic News,* July 8th, 1939."

"Several deceased friends addressed sitters by name and in every case correctly defined their exact degree of relationship.

"At the second séance I took my mother. Mr Webber did not know my mother was present, yet my father spoke and addressed her with a favourite expression of hers. The tone and inflexion was undoubtedly my father's, so much so, that my mother, who is extremely sceptical, instantly recognized it.

"The roping was carried out by a post-office engineer . . . My little son spoke to me, with and without the trumpet, he afterwards materialized within five inches of my face . . . my little boy asked for his Mummy and spoke about a bottle. Asked, 'What bottle?' He said: 'Don't you remember? You put it in my hand when I was in the coffin.' His mother broke down on hearing his voice. I asked him: 'Where were you when that happened?' He said: 'Standing by Mummy's side.' Now I knew nothing of this incident, but on questioning my wife, I found she had put a small bottle of perfume in his hand the day before the funeral.

.   .   .   .   .

" . . . there is no possible doubt that the voice which addressed me through a trumpet floating at some distance from Webber's chair was my dead father's voice . . . my father's voice was very distinctive and unmistakable. He was a man of three Universities, a member of the professional class, and a man of culture. His speech, voice, enunciation, and intonation were typical. Mr Webber's voice is that of a working man and a provincial.

" *Two Worlds,* March 3rd, 1939."

"The Guide said he would dematerialize the medium, and before our eyes, in good red light, we saw the head, hands, and wrists vanish, leaving just the medium's clothes in the chair. It remained so for approximately a minute. We all then saw the rapid emergence of the medium.

"*Two Worlds*, March 3rd, 1939."

CHAPTER XIX

THE GUIDES' CARE OF THE MEDIUM

MR WEBBER sits about two hundred times a year, including public sittings and his developing circle. He has never ceased to sit for his own further development. It is in this developing circle that the Guides are preparing to demonstrate in red light, to develop further the physical materializations of spirit people, and to conduct their own experiments to improve their technique for these demonstrations.

Every possible precaution is taken to protect the medium from accident. During this large number of sittings, accidents do sometimes occur. Occasionally some person unwittingly interferes with an article still connected with the medium by an ectoplasmic arm or rod. In one instance, in the developing circle, whilst four trumpets were in levitation, a sitter's arm, on which a trumpet temporarily had come to rest, was moved. When such events occur there is bleeding from the medium's mouth and nose, and once when somebody deliberately shone a light on to the medium there was external bleeding from the solar plexus. It may be that the interference has been slight and phenomena have continued after bleeding, but as a rule the sitting terminates.

The medium has also been unconscious for considerable periods. Black Cloud has explained that he has to "leave the body to permit the return of the medium's astral body. If the condition of the physical body was such that the astral body could not return, the medium would pass over."

During these periods, especially during the unconscious state, the controls are administering healing to the body. On one occasion such as this, when after a séance a period of unconsciousness ensued, the sitters present tried various remedies without success. The voice of Black Cloud was then heard, telling the people to leave the medium alone.

Latterly, when mishaps have occurred and a state of unconsciousness has ensued, Black Cloud has re-entered the body and brought Mr Webber back to normality. It is noteworthy that on such occasions Mr Webber feels but slight ill-effect from the incident.

At a sitting when the photographers of the *Daily Mirror* were in attendance, endeavouring to obtain a photograph of the medium roped to his chair in levitation, a mishap took place. Instead of the Guide asking for "photograph" he said, "Light," and the one in charge of the white light did not put it on. Again came the command, in imperative tones: "Put the light on," and it was put on. The medium was seen to be in the air some distance from the floor. A major calamity was feared. Then the sitters saw the medium *descend in slow motion,* turning a complete somersault as he descended, arriving on the floor on his head, the chair being upside down, and his feet uppermost. The medium and chair were stood upright by the sitters, and after a state of unconsciousness of about twenty minutes, normality returned. No harm or ill-effect was felt by the medium. Strangest of all is that there was no bruise on the head, or even a red mark, where his head came into contact with the floor. (See "Trumpet Phenomena" for similar non-injury.)

Mr Webber tells of an experience he had as a miner. He was engaged on repair work, by himself, in a mine some two miles away from the main shaft, when his lamp failed. In the low tortuous windings of the mine passages it was almost impossible for any person in the dark to find his way out. Mr Webber tells how a small blue light appeared in front of his face and guided him through the passages to the main shaft, where his workmates would not believe his story. This event occurred sometime before Mr Webber had any knowledge of his psychic powers.

The following point can never be stressed too much or too often to people who attend séances of this nature. Never commit any unorthodox action, or interfere with any phase of the phenomena, or touch any article in levitation or after levitation. The medium's life may be imperilled by such action. The photographs show the nature of the forces used, but if also the strength used for various feats is considered, the harm that would be caused to a medium by the uncontrolled return of these forces to the physical body must be immediately apparent. Interference may perhaps kill the medium, or at least destroy health, sight, and the powers of mediumship. No research experiment should ever be contemplated without the full knowledge and co-operation of the Guide in control.

Author's Personal Note.—The author was walking home one evening heavily laden with awkward parcels, and unthinkingly crossed a main road immediately on turning a corner, walking across the road obliquely. When half-way across he received a sudden impetuous urge to gain the pavement at all costs. No sooner had he achieved this than a coal motor lorry travelling at speed came round the corner. Without any doubt, the writer would have been in serious difficulties had he not felt impelled to take quick action to get off the roadway.

There have been other occasions when persons associated with Mr Webber have been helped out of difficulties.

CHAPTER XX

ELECTRICAL INTERFERENCES

A NUMBER of unexplained incidents have occurred during séances in which electrical apparatus has been interfered with and other happenings have taken place that may have a bearing upon the employment of electrical forces by the spirit people.

One evening, preparations had been made to take photographs by the usual infra-red apparatus. Battery, connections, leads, etc., were overhauled, checked, and found to be in order. During the séance, when instructions were given to take a photograph, the bulbs would not fire. When the séance was over, each bulb that refused to fire was placed in the light cabinet and on contact being made they flashed at once.

At Leeds Psychic Research Society, a similar experience was noted. After a failure of the first bulb to flash, the white light was put on, a new battery was installed, and the firing points checked. The séance proceeded, yet no bulb would flash. At one time an unexplained light was seen near the apparatus.

The strength of the red light in the medium's developing circle has often been varied without human contact with the rheostat.

After an incident at another sitting, when the electric light had been put on, the fuse controlling the lights in another part of the house was put out of order.

In the two latter cases, there is evidence of direct manipulation of a fuse and the intensity of light, which apparently could be altered as desired.

The contrary happened with the first two cases cited, and perhaps also happened in connection with the incident that follows. Obviously, the medium's controls would not take the trouble to prepare a phenomenon to be photographed, only to render their own efforts abortive by interference. It is logical that other spirit intelligences conducting research work of their own have been responsible for the occurrences. At times the medium's control has asked us to disconnect apparatus as other presences were likely to interfere. When it is considered, admitting the presence of the controls with the medium, it is only reasonable to assume that other independent intelligences can also be present and indeed that they would take advantage of the opportunity in a physical séance; where apparatus exists, for the purpose of conducting their own personal "tests".

A remarkable incident occurred at Wolverhampton in January 1940. A séance had been in progress for a while when a flash of bright light was seen by all sitters coming from a levitated trumpet, which immediately crashed to the floor. The Guide at once asked for light, when the medium was found to be unconscious and bleeding from the nose and finger-nails.

The organizer of the séance, a Mr Herbert Wright, also a medium, was in charge of the light-switch, standing outside the circle of sitters. As the flash came, he received a terrific blow in the solar plexus region. As he reeled, he heard the Guide ask for light, which he was just able to switch on before becoming unconscious. It is definitely ascertained that Mr Wright did not put the light on and was in no way normally responsible for the flash that was seen near the medium.

During the ten minutes during which Mr Wright was unconscious, no respiration could be noted, and clouds of steam arose from his body. When he recovered consciousness, his garments were saturated with perspiration, and a mark, generally termed a "psychic burn," encircled his body. This mark was red in colour and threequarters of an inch wide, commencing at the solar plexus and travelling right round the body and ending where it began. This band was extremely painful, yet the main trouble experienced by Mr Wright was in other nerve centres of his body.

The author spoke to the Guide about this incident a few days later, and Black Cloud gave the opinion that the incident was caused through a joining up of the force created through the mediumship with the positive wire in an electric pendant, near the medium's head.

This is the first occasion recorded with Mr Webber where the "power" was "earthed" back to another person, and there is little doubt that had this not been the case, Mr Webber would have suffered severely.

CHAPTER XXI

CONCLUSIONS

MANY questions will arise in the mind of the reader who has read the foregoing chapters. To those convinced of the reality of survival, little more need be added, for they will recognize the operation of the wonderful powers of the spirit people, and while marvelling at them, will understand them.

To the reader not so convinced some perplexity is inevitable. At the risk of redundancy, it may be repeated that the whole of the incidents related have occurred recently. That the mediumship of Mr Webber is still with us. That demonstrations can be witnessed, and photographs taken.

It should be made plain that while it would not be possible to accommodate every individual photographer or enquirer desiring satisfaction for a particular type of phenomenon, every effort will be made to afford facilities for investigation to any *bona fide* association.

The pertinent fact is that every statement made dealing with the séance work, and every photograph taken, are capable of being re-demonstrated. [1]

This statement is stressed to meet the only possible criticism that, in spite of the independent corroboration, the phenomena described are the product of imagination, and that a conspiracy embracing hundreds of people and impartial organizations has produced "staged" photographs.

---

1. Written before the decease of the medium. It must be emphasized that there are other mediums through whose agency similar phenomena may be witnessed.

If the reader accepts the evidence that the supernormal activities did take place, the following observations may be helpful in arriving at a fundamental decision.

1. Each phenomenon is a deliberate act, planned from its commencement to its completion.

2. To produce phenomena, law-governed forces are employed.

3. To produce phenomena consciously, or subconsciously, is beyond human effort, mental or physical.

4. To employ forces within man's knowledge intelligent direction is required.

5. To employ spirit-forces, intelligent direction is also required.

6. The execution of an act of phenomena demands the application and combination of both spirit agencies and physical forces.

7. To have gained such knowledge the operating intelligence can only have obtained wisdom through experience and thought activity. This experience has not been gained through human effort and therefore cannot be the product of the sub-conscious mind.

8. It is reasonable to accept verbal evidence of survival co-existent with the phenomena as part of the phenomena.

9. It is reasonable to accept that a form of existence continues after "death" through the re-creation in physical forms of persons who have passed over, together with the ability to recognize and be recognized, and to converse intelligently about common memories.

These observations lead to this question:

What can be the nature of the directing intelligence able to control and direct both the spirit and physical forces? Logic affirms that it must of necessity be a discarnate or spirit intelligence. This is further demonstrated when it is considered

*that this intelligence must be in touch with other spirit people
in order to provide for them the means to communicate through
human mediumship. Logic also affirms that there must be a
further period of individual activity after the earthly phase of
existence.*

This brings us back to the Foreword of this book in which its
purpose was clearly stated: to demonstrate that survival is a
truth—a proven fact. If this book does so, its purpose has been
achieved and the change in our code of values must follow.

CHAPTER XXII

THE "RETURN" OF JACK WEBBER

A stated in the Obituary Notice, Jack Webber passed into spirit-life on March 9th, 1940, at 9.30a.m.

On Sunday, March 10th, at the Wandsworth branch of the Marylebone Spiritualist Association, Mrs Bertha Harris was the medium conducting the evening service.

After the meeting she mentioned that during the service she felt she was surrounded by trumpets moving about. Then came the name of Jack Webber with the impression that he wanted to get in touch with Harry (the author). It so happened that the author was present at that service but owing to a late arrival had to be content with a seat in the annexe, as the church was packed, and he left without speaking to anyone.

There was also present a lady who knew that the medium had passed on, and after the service told Mrs Harris what had happened, which explained the presence of the trumpets and the message which Mrs Harris could not understand at the time of its reception.

.   .   .   .   .

On Tuesday, March 12th, at Hendon Spiritualist Fellowship, where Mr Webber had demonstrated on his first visit to London, and where, by the invitation of the President of the church, Mrs Catherine Wilson, the author first witnessed the mediumship, little comprehending the events that were to follow, of which this book is the result, a medium, Miss Eveline Cannon, was demonstrating clairvoyance when she saw Mr Webber.

Not knowing that Mr Webber had passed on, and believing him to be physically alive, she could not understand the vision she saw. Miss Cannon relates that Mr Webber, observing her dilemma, shook his head and disappeared. It was only afterwards when discussing this matter with Mrs Wilson that she heard for the first time of the passing.

.   .   .   .   .

On the evening of the same day, at a developing circle held for direct voice at the Great Metropolitan Spiritualist Association, a trumpet was levitated through the mediumship of Mr Harold Evans, and Jack Webber spoke. Mr Webber had demonstrated a number of times at this society, and amongst those present were a number of persons who had known Mr Webber well. Apart from the message (characteristic of him), the sitters recognized the tonal qualities of his voice, so that the value of the communication was evidential.

.   .   .   .   .

On Wednesday, another medium, Mr Harold Sharp, saw Jack Webber clairvoyantly with a company of other people, one of whom he recognized as a Mrs Lander, a great friend of Mr Webber's, who had passed over a few months previously. To Mr Sharp's vision Mr Webber held up to him a baby. Five weeks before Mr Webber's passing, he had attended the funeral of a baby niece. Mr Sharp was unaware of this incident.

.   .   .   .   .

On the next day, Thursday, after the body had been interred, preparations had been made for a service for members of the family and the developing circle, in the house, in the evening. The chairs had been arranged, and the only light was that from a coal fire. Mr Webber senior, an elderly gentleman, not a strong spiritualist, entered the room with the idea of having a short rest.

As he opened the door he saw his son Jack standing in the room, and instinctively stepped forward—not comprehending—and shook hands with his son. As he did so, the realization of what he was doing overcame him, and made him so distraught that he was indisposed for some hours afterwards. Mr Webber senior says he saw his son as if he were "really there", and felt his hand as he shook hands.

.   .   .   .   .

During the period of the following two weeks (to the date when this is being written) many other reports have been received from mediums who testify that Mr Webber has made himself known through their mediumship, but the above will serve as sufficient evidence that Mr Webber has returned. It will be noted in all the above cases that he returned to people who knew him well, whom he liked, and in three cases gave evidence before the medium concerned knew of the passing.

His family and friends have naturally asked why, with all Jack's protective influences, attendant healers, and spirit-helpers, he should have been taken away so quickly. That question cannot be answered now, but it may yet be answered with evidence, by the new work he may undertake, in his new sphere of activity—to prove survival—of which the incidents narrated may be a criterion of that to come.

CHAPTER XXIII

THE AUTHOR—HENRY JAMES (HARRY) EDWARDS

BORN 1893 of London parents. Educated at Noel Park School, Wood Green.

From an early age displayed an interest in public work. At the age of fifteen pioneered one of the first Boy Scout troops. Later became interested in political work as a Liberal, and at eighteen became a secretary of a Liberal Association.

During the Great War he first undertook work on behalf of the Belgian Relief Fund and the Prince of Wales National Relief Fund. Enlisted in November 1914, in The Royal Sussex Regiment. Saw service in India, where he took up an active interest in the social welfare work for the military and founded and edited the Royal Sussex Herald.

Commissioned in the field in Baghdad in 1918, obtained rank of captain in 1920, with post of Director of Labour for North-West Persia.

After demobilization founded a printing and stationery business and continued his work in the social and political sphere. Was founder and executive officer of ex-servicemen's associations and branches of the League of Nations' Union.

Contested parliamentary elections, North Camberwell, 1929; North West Camberwell, 1936, and also the London County Council Elections on four occasions.

Commenced investigation into spiritualism in 1936. Sat for personal development, and became quickly aware of healing powers, and trance speech and clairvoyance.

Mr Edwards first saw Mr Webber at his first visit to London in April 1938 at Hendon.

During the next four months Mr Webber paid three visits to circles arranged by Mr Edwards. On the last occasion, in early September, Mr George Daisley, the well-known medium, was present previous to a sitting, and Daisley, Webber, and Edwards were together in the séance room. Mr Daisley jokingly expressed a desire to see how it felt to be roped in a chair, and he was so secured. He then said his Guide would like to come and speak, and he submitted himself for control. His Guide, Tomaso, spoke and told Mr Webber that there would be great and new developments for him in that room, and, turning to Mr Edwards, said he would write a book about them.

At that time no word had been said regarding Mr Webber coming to London, and the message was accepted with considerable reserve.

A few weeks later Mr Webber wrote to Mr Edwards and said he wanted to come and live in London and asked for suitable premises to be found. At first the efforts were unsuccessful, and then on an inspiration Mr Edwards asked his next-door neighbours if they would think of moving. He was told that they wished to, and within a month the house was vacated, and Mr Webber and his people were installed.

The work has gone on in the same séance room, the new development of photographic records has been taken, and the book is written.

ADDENDUM, MARCH 1940.

The next time Mr George Daisley came to the author's house was in January, 1940, for the purpose of giving advice, by his Guide, to Mrs Layton, concerning her personal development. Mr Daisley asked the author and Mrs Edwards to sit with Mrs Layton.

Tomaso, the Guide, entranced Mr Daisley, and during the time he was present turned to the author and referred to his previous prophecy, which had come true. Tomaso continued saying words to the effect that there would be a disappointment with the book, but that would disappear. He then said, there is a great sorrow to come, and the parting between you and Mr Webber will be brought about as quickly as you came together.

Again, the author was sceptical, and did not pay much heed to the new prophecy, for then its fulfilment seemed most remote, but again it has happened, the parting, in physical life, has taken place, with the abruptness described.

Did the spirit people have pre-knowledge of Mr Webber's passing? Who can say? Suffice it that each prophecy (unacceptable at the time) has proven true.

We only realize the lack of our knowledge and comprehension of spirit activity the deeper we delve into it. There is obviously a boundary we cannot pass, but out of the mists of obscurity we are able to place together a few factual fragments, preparing the way for the greater knowledge of the future; certain at least of the sure foundation, that there is no "death", but a new phase of individual existence, greater than any we can now conceive.

THE END

www.ingramcontent.com/pod-product-compliance
Lightning Source LLC
LaVergne TN
LVHW051126080426
835510LV00018B/2258